# TO GET A BETTER SCHOOL SYSTEM

**NUMBER 111:**

*Centennial Series of the Association of Former Students,*
*Texas A&M University*

# To Get a Better School System

## One Hundred Years of Education Reform in Texas

*Gene B. Preuss*

Texas A&M University Press

*College Station*

Copyright © 2009 by Gene B. Preuss
Manufactured in the United States of America
All rights reserved
First edition
This paper meets the requirements of ANSI/NISO Z39.48-1992
(Permanence of Paper).
Binding materials have been chosen for durability.

Library of Congress Cataloging-in-Publication Data
Preuss, Gene B., 1966–
To get a better school system : one hundred years of education
reform in Texas / Gene B. Preuss. — 1st ed.
p. cm. — (Centennial series of the Association of Former
Students, Texas A&M University ; no. 111)
Includes bibliographical references and index.
ISBN-13: 978-1-60344-111-7 (cloth : alk. paper)
ISBN-10: 1-60344-111-5 (cloth : alk. paper)
1. Educational change—Texas—History. 2. Education and state—Texas—
History. 3. Minorities—Education—Texas—History. 4. Education, Rural—
Texas—History. 5. Gilmer-Aikin laws, 1949. I. Title. II. Series: Centennial series
of the Association of Former Students, Texas A&M University ; no. 111.
LA370.P74 2009
379.764'0904—dc22
2008050656

Frontis and p. xii: Children in a schollroom in San
Augustine, 1943. Courtesy Library of Congress

FOR EUGENE & ISABEL, AND MARI

# TABLE OF CONTENTS

# PREFACE

When historians write about reform movements, the resulting works are often administrative studies evaluating the way a bureaucracy forms and operates. Policy studies, comparing and contrasting the differences between the expectations the reformers promised and those that actually resulted either because of limits owing to racism or economic opportunism, are another popular approach. Histories of reform are sometimes cultural studies, viewing the reform as the imposition of one culture upon another. Educational historians such as Michael Katz, David Tyack, and Diane Ravitch have effectively addressed school reforms using these perspectives.

The story of school reform in Texas allows us to evaluate school reform from a different perspective. Instead of a policy analysis or an evaluation of the success or shortcomings of the policy, the purpose of this study is to uncover the reasons why Texas lawmakers initiated a dramatic change in the state's public school administration following World War II, especially when legislators had previously rejected substantially the same reforms on previous occasions. It is my contention that Texans had always wanted a first-rate system of education, but only the threat of a crisis moved Texans to look beyond strong political and economic prejudices that led them to oppose earlier reform suggestions. Reformers advocated a centralized system of tax-supported public education, while opponents held that education was a parental responsibility and worried that too much centralization threatened local control.

Americans, like people in other cultures, are willing to make drastic changes when they perceive a threat, and in recent years the fear of an impending national crisis has often precipitated educational reform. In the late 1950s, Sputnik threatened U.S. military security, and in the 1980s, *A Nation at Risk* warned of a cultural and economic crisis. In both cases, the nation looked toward education as a means of preserving the American way of life.

In 1949, likewise, reformers successfully used the recent world war to persuade the public that a centralized school system would preserve democracy and that the money spent on education would be in Texas' best interest.

Although the events and circumstances that led to the change in attitude were complex and diverse, reformers used a simple argument that appealed to the populist and democratic ideals of rural Texans: public education is an equalizing force that will preserve democracy, and every school child should have a good education.

# Acknowledgments

Sir Isaac Newton once wrote, "If I have seen further, it is by standing on the shoulders of giants." Although I certainly would never compare myself with a genius such as Newton, I certainly believe that our successes are dependent upon the assistance of others. This study began as a dissertation under the direction of Alwyn Barr at Texas Tech University; he along with Paul Carlson, Donald Walker, Otto Nelson, and Jorge Iber were true teachers, scholars, and friends. David Murrah, Ty Cashion, Mark Barringer, Carlos Blanton, and Bill Griggs provided constant encouragement, as well.

I appreciate the special help provided by the dedicated staff at Texas Tech's Southwest Collection/Special Collection Library, especially Janet Neugebauer and Tai Kreidler. Jim Conrad at the James G. Gee Library Archive at Texas A&M–Commerce allowed me tremendous access to the papers of A. M. Aikin Jr. Jean Carefoot at the Texas State Archives searched for several years for boxes that Rae Files Still deposited in the archive in the 1950s. Although she was unsuccessful and the missing boxes eventually turned up in 2005 at the Center for American History, she deserves credit for maintaining a search with an archivist's tenacity. Douglas Weiskopf at the Texas and Local History Department of the Houston Public Library was also helpful.

Mary Lenn Dixon, at Texas A&M University Press, has been a patient guide through the publication process. Thom Lemmons, copyeditor Scott Barker, and the two anonymous readers provided welcome suggestions.

Fred Allison, Page Foshee, Shawn Fonville, Dan Pacious, Chuck Waite, Scott Sosebee, Michael James, Joe Westfall, John Linantud, Jim Rutledge, and Fr. Mike Van Cleve have been wonderful friends, providing encouragement and frequent humility checks.

My parents, Eugene and Isabel, always encouraged me to "get all the education you can," and by their sacrifice and support they provided me with an education they could not receive. This book is therefore dedicated to them.

Finally, Mari L. Nicholson-Preuss has been a wonderful partner, wife, colleague, and soul mate. She has sustained, supported, and tolerated me for the past ten years. She deserves more than I can ever repay, but I hope the dedication will demonstrate how important she has been in my life.

Despite the best efforts of all the people I have mentioned, and many I have omitted, I bear full responsibility for any error, omission, or shortcoming of the work that follows.

# To Get a Better School System

# INTRODUCTION

In January 1946, the Texas State Teachers Association (TSTA) newsletter, the *Texas Outlook,* mourned the death of Annie Webb Blanton, who had passed away October 2, 1945.[1] Blanton served as the TSTA's first woman president in 1916, and the first woman to be state superintendent of public instruction from 1919 to 1923. While she was state superintendent, she led a public school reform movement known as the "Better Schools Campaign" from 1919 to 1920. The *Outlook* noted that the TSTA's Resolutions Subcommittee passed a resolution which urged that "the Legislature of Texas continue to make provisions for increasing teachers' salaries to the level comparable to that paid other professions."[2] Blanton's obituary seemed to mark a transition from one phase of public school reform in Texas to another.

Three years later, the Texas legislature passed three bills that completely reorganized the state's public education system. The bills, known collectively as the Gilmer-Aikin Bills, comprised the most comprehensive public school reform in Texas history and had an effect upon "the entire school system of the state—pupils, teachers, school administrators, parents, school districts, cities, counties, and taxpayers."[3] The Gilmer-Aikin program marked one of the major turning points in Texas educational history.

Despite the sweeping changes brought about by the Gilmer-Aikin reforms, the extant literature on them is small. Aside from one early book that chronicled the legislative process behind the bills, there is no work specifically devoted to the history of the school reform bills. Moreover, the last comprehensive text on Texas public education history was written over fifty years ago. There is little scholarship that addresses the success reformers had in passing the Gilmer-Aikin reforms. Despite the legislation's vast change to the state's educational system, these reforms have received little attention, until recently. For example, one history text could only state that "the best evaluation of the Gilmer-Aikin acts would be that they at least moved the state educational system into the early twentieth century."[4]

There are two sides to the debate over school reform. On the one hand, proponents of school reform pointed to the poor state of public education before the reformist impulse of the late nineteenth- and early twentieth-century Progressive Era. These historians painted a gloomy portrait of the state of the public school system and implied that without reforms, schools would atrophy and this would lead to the ruin of the people and economic development of the state. According to this viewpoint, educational reformers were heroic figures fighting against entrenched politics and traditions to create a better environment for school children to grow and develop. Others have pointed to the need for true school reform in the face of increasing technology, population, and industry in the state following World War II. Ellwood P. Cubberley, writing in the Progressive Era, laid the groundwork for this perspective, and Lawrence A. Cremin's *The Transformation of the School* is foremost in this school of thought.[5]

On the other hand, more recent critics charge that reformers sought to impose urban, middle-class ideals upon tight-knit rural communities. David Tyack's *The One Best System* focused on the changes from "localism" toward "professionalism." William A. Link applied this viewpoint to his work on Virginia school reform in *A Hard Country and a Lonely Place* and later to a general regional assessment titled *Paradox of Southern Progressivism*. Link sees reformers as bureaucratic outsiders challenging local traditionalists for power. The most recent criticism of school reform appears in Diane Ravitch's *Left Back,* wherein she argues that Progressive-era reformers actually undermined the democratization of U.S. education. By promoting a curriculum designed around a child's individual needs, she writes, poor and minority children were "pushed into undemanding vocational, industrial, or general programs by bureaucrats and guidance counselors who thought they were incapable of learning much more."[6]

There are only two comprehensive works on Texas public schools. Frederick Eby, professor of education at the University of Texas, published *Education in Texas* in 1925. Cecil Eugene Evans, president of Southwest Texas State Teachers College, wrote *The Story of Texas Schools* in 1955. No new comprehensive study of Texas public education has emerged in the half century since Evans's book. Most of the recent works pertaining to Texas public schools have been brief, journalistic articles in the *Texas Outlook,* and there have been several works based on oral histories that offer a nostalgic look at the days of the one-room schoolhouse. These include *Ringing the Children In,* by Thad Sitton and Milam C. Rowold, and Luther Bryan Clegg's *The Empty Schoolhouse.* Desegregation and equalization for minority schools have gained some increased attention. Guadalupe San Miguel Jr.'s *"Let All of Them Take Heed": Mexican Americans and the Campaign for Educational Equality in Texas, 1910–1981* is a comprehensive look at the Mexican American experience in Texas. He also examines efforts to prohibit the Houston ISD from integrating Mexican American students in *Brown, Not White: School Integration and the Chicano Movement in Houston.* Robyn Duff Landino's *Desegregating Texas Schools: Eisenhower, Shivers, and the Crisis at Mansfield High,* and William Henry Kellar's *Make Haste Slowly: Moderates, Conservatives, and School Desegregation in Houston* have examined desegregation for African American students in two locales. Carlos Blanton's *The Strange Career of Bilingual Education in Texas, 1836–1981* reveals that assimilationist trends during the Progressive Era and in the post–World War I generation contributed to an English-only policy in Texas public schools that remained in force until challenged when former Texas schoolteacher-turned-president Lyndon Johnson signed the Bilingual Education Act in 1968.[7]

Although Gilmer-Aikin led to important reforms, studies of the legislation are limited. Aside from passing discussions in survey Texas history texts, there is little that evaluates the effects of the Gilmer-Aikin reforms on public education and considers the place of public school reform in the larger context of Texas history. There is only one work specifically devoted to a comprehensive examination of the school reform bills, their origins, and immediate results. In 1950, shortly after the passage of the legislation, state representative Rae Files Still of Waxahachie, who chaired the House Committee on Education, published a history of the actions that led to the passage of the bills. Originally prepared as a master's thesis in political science, her book, *The Gilmer-Aikin Laws,* provides readers with an insider's account of the committee investigations, the drafting of the legislation, as well as the parliamentary manipulation and behind-the-scenes maneuvering.[8]

Education students at Texas universities also produced several theses detailing the effects of Gilmer-Aikin on various school districts around the state. Written soon after the bills' passage, these early attempts to chart the influences of the reform measures upon the state's public schools lack an historical evaluation of their significance. In addition, these works look at the immediate effects of Gilmer-Aikin from educational or political science instead of historical perspectives. But, they do provide detailed examinations of the execution of the reform in specific school districts around the state. A synthesis of these works will help evaluate the historical significance Gilmer-Aikin had in different school districts across the state.

Resources previously unavailable to researchers have been opened in recent years. For example, the A. M. and Welma Aikin Regional Archive at Paris Junior College, and the A. M. Aikin Jr. legislative papers at Texas A&M University-Commerce contain information relating to Aikin's service in the legislature, including his work on the committee and the laws that bear his name. The Texas State Library and Archives house the papers of the state's school superintendents, the Texas Education Agency, and the committees on education in the state legislature, as well as various speech files by Texas governors. The Texas State Teachers Association's monthly journal, *Texas Outlook,* contains much information regarding the effects of the Gilmer-Aikin reforms beyond the time period covered by the early theses and dissertations.

Oral history interviews conducted to supplement the Aikin papers in Commerce also shed new light on the history and effects of the laws. Other oral history collections throughout the state contain interviews with public school teachers and administrators from the period. While Seth Shepard McKay used several of the state's major newspapers in his brief discussion of the Gilmer-Aikin reforms, he did not refer to minority publications. Neither did he make use of letters to the editor. Because Gilmer-Aikin received little historical attention, many of these sources have gone unexamined. The use of these sources provides insight into how the public responded to the changes in the public schools and increases in taxes and teachers' salaries. Minority papers provide an insight into how the reforms and school consolidations affected black and Hispanic teachers and pupils.

This study explores the political, social, and economic environment of Texas following World War II and the impulse for public educational reform. The war challenged Americans' perceptions of racial relations, the states' relations to the nation, the population and prosperity of the nation, and the place of the United States in world events. These issues influenced education as well. During the war, the draft illuminated the need for standardized education and health services in schools. After the war, the baby boom and the cold war also demanded expansion of school services and the need for an improved, standardized curriculum.

These events also affected Texans. Texas cities grew after the war as people increasingly moved into the South and Southwest. Forecasters predicted a great increase in school-age children by the 1950s. The battle over the Tidelands seemed a rallying point for legislators—a means of getting more money for education without increased taxation. Participation in World War II also began to raise concerns over the racial situation in the United States. In fighting against a racist regime, the nation could not easily condone racism at home. Texans also wondered how to improve a segregated educational system and how to increase educational quality without increasing spending. How lawmakers resolved these problems would affect minority students and children living in poor and rural districts.

Gilmer-Aikin seemed to answer many of the questions concerning the needed changes in education. At the same time, the laws challenged traditional Texans' philosophies about the sanctity of locally controlled schools and decentralized education systems. George N. Green, in *The Establishment in Texas Politics,* suggested that the primary reason for the reform was to oust State Superintendent L. A. Woods. Recent oral histories of rural schools have glorified the "good old days" of the one-room schoolhouse. They complain that rural school consolidation, accelerated by Gilmer-Aikin, destroyed the community school and threatened local control of the public schools in favor of the gospel of efficiency and centralization. This study hopes to demonstrate the influences and importance of the cultural and social developments in Texas following World War II on changing attitudes toward school reform that resulted in the passage of Gilmer-Aikin.[9]

The chronological organization of this study demonstrates historical development of the state's school system. Chapter 1 examines the importance public education took on in Texas and the South following the period of the Civil War and Reconstruction to the end of the nineteenth century. Chapter 2 carries the history of Texas public education into the mid-twentieth century. The chapter examines the state of public schools in Texas up to the onset of World War II. Some of the questions I hope to answer include: How much had Texas schools progressed since the turn of the century? Why did a major difference develop between urban and rural schools? Who led the movement to reform public education?

Chapter 3 examines the economic, social, and political changes that developed after World War II. The development of the civil rights movement affected a large number of Americans after the war, yet the changes to end educational segregation that culminated in the *Brown* decision in 1954 originated during the 1940s. This chapter will evaluate the public school experiences of Mexican American and African American school children in Texas, the struggle for equalization of teachers' salaries, and the effects of World War II in easing racial discrimination.

Chapter 4 will examine how World War II influenced national trends in education, especially the need for improved school services, health education and physical training, and a more standardized educational curriculum. The primary focus will be the renewed emphasis on the role of education in preserving democracy. Yet as the gaps in rural education became more obvious, rural schools across the nation faced consolidation as a solution. State representatives from rural areas and their constituents began to perceive inadequacies in their local schools. As Texas became an urban state, rural communities found themselves supporting school consolidation, a measure they had previously opposed, to preserve their dwindling communities.

The political origins and development of Gilmer-Aikin will be considered in chapter 5. But the primary focus of the chapter will be the political battle between the state superintendent of public instruction, Littleton A. Woods, and Texas state senator A. M. Aikin over the significant changes that Gilmer-Aikin represented. Finally, chapter 6 will consider the long-range results of the reforms.

This book seeks to demonstrate that the trend toward increased centralization that Gilmer-Aikin embodied evolved from progressive educational reforms already occurring in the Texas and other southern states. These bills sought to make better use of the increasing money requested by one-room rural schools. Further, the laws aimed to standardize the curriculum in the state's public schools and to improve conditions and professionalize training for public school teachers.

# Chapter 1
# RETREAT AND RECOVERY
# IN TEXAS SCHOOLS, 1850–1900

The idea of free public education was gaining popularity in the early 1820s when American and European settlers came to Mexican Texas to take advantage of the liberal immigration policies provided by the new government of the Republic of Mexico. When Stephen F. Austin built his colony in southeast Texas, he vigorously supported the establishment of a system of public education in his colonial capital of San Felipe de Austin.[1] Although other private schools operated, Austin wanted a permanent, publicly supported school for the colony. While the concept of free public education was important to settlers in early Texas, the establishment of a system of schools throughout the state took many years to accomplish because the solution to funding public education eluded early nineteenth-century educational supporters. Like the proponents of state-supported public education elsewhere, Republic of Texas leaders planned to fund education with the sale of public lands. Unfortunately, the problem of relying upon the sale of land proved unworkable because the Texas government sold available land for only fifty cents an acre, two and a half times less than the United States charged settlers, in order to attract emigrants into the region. Considering the large amount of land given away to those who immigrated or served in the Texas Revolution, the republic gained little money for education from land sales. Limited funds and serious opposition to increased taxation stymied attempts to establish public education throughout the South, leading one author to characterize school laws as "a record of beautifully phrased plans that never materialized."[2]

Furthermore, those who supported free public education remained a small minority. While Texans supported free public education for orphans and indigent children, expanding this benefit to all children would have proved too costly. Cecil E. Evans wrote, "There was no sentiment in the Republic of Texas for school taxation." He further explained, "Any attempt at this time to establish public free schools under laws and regulations similar to those of the twentieth century would have been condemned as tyranny."[3]

Once Texas became a state, it again addressed the idea of establishing a system of public education. The Constitution of 1845 echoed the belief in the necessity of education for the preservation of a republic. "A general diffusion of knowledge being essential to the preservation of the rights and liberties of the people," section 10 began, "it shall be the duty of the legislature of this State to make suitable provisions for the support and maintenance of public schools." The constitution further stipulated that a property tax would finance the school system, in addition to 10 percent of the annual state revenue that would be set aside to establish a permanent fund to support the school system.[4] Few public schools, however, ever emerged from this provision under the state's first constitution.

When Texas relinquished its claims on Santa Fe and the New Mexico Territory as a part of the Compromise of 1850, the state received ten million dollars in exchange. The windfall paid for the state debt incurred during the Texas Revolution, and the balance gave state leaders the opportunity to support much needed public improvements, especially in transportation and public education. The legislature enacted the School Law of 1854 and set aside almost two million dollars for the permanent school fund, but it then loaned money from the fund to finance railroad construction within the state. The legislature believed that by investing the school fund in railroads the interest from these loans would go to further the amount of money in the public education fund.[5]

In less than a decade, however, the educational plans of the legislature were shattered. The railroad companies, notorious for going bankrupt because of the tremendous amount of capital needed for rolling stock, iron rails, laborers, and operating costs, defaulted. Additionally, the Civil War bankrupted the state's hope of sustaining itself through Cotton Diplomacy because of the Union blockade of the Gulf Coast, combined with political instability in Mexico that restricted the trade with the textile mills of Great Britain and Europe. With a depleted school fund and the economic and manpower demands of the war, public schooling in Texas came to a halt. Efforts to bring a comprehensive public education system to Texas children had to wait for the sectional conflict to end—and for Reconstruction to begin.

## PUBLIC EDUCATION AFTER THE CIVIL WAR

With the success of the Union forces over the Confederacy, Texas began the process of Reconstruction. In the early months of 1866, a convention met to draft a new state constitution. The men chosen reflected a conservative mindset. Oran M. Roberts, the leader of the secession convention, was now a member of the constitutional convention. While the new constitution conceded basic human rights to the freedmen, it severely abridged their rights of citizenship, even denying African Americans the right to public education. The Republicans in the United States Congress balked at the attempts of Texas and other former Confederate states to allow former Confederates to resume their previous political offices and at the legal chicanery aimed at keeping African Americans in a status similar to slavery. Congress therefore commissioned the War Department's Bureau of Refugees, Freedmen, and Abandoned Lands, or Freedmen's Bureau, to assist former slaves with their adjustment from slavery to freedom.

The Bureau established schools in response to their wards' demand for education to overcome the widespread illiteracy mandated under slavery. Under the direction of the Texas superintendent of public instruction, Edwin M. Wheelock, the Freedmen's Bureau established sixteen schools in 1865 with 1,041 enrolled students. The next year, according to Texas Freedmen's Bureau historian Barry Crouch, the Bureau supervised ninety schools, including private African American schools, day and night schools, and Sunday schools, serving nearly 4,600 students (including over 1,700 adults) with 43 teachers, one-third of which were African American. Despite white opposition, cholera and yellow fever epidemics, the difficulty in recruiting teachers, natural disasters, and the demand for laborers, Bureau schools reported 3,248 students enrolled in its sixty-six schools when the Freedmen's Bureau discontinued operation in 1871.[6]

Violence against students and teachers was one of the most serious obstacles threatening Bureau schools. After the war ended, political control remained in the hands of the Southern establishment. Texans ignored Confederate Postmaster General John H. Reagan's advice that they acquiesce to Northern expectations following the war and "adopt a plan which will fully meet the demands of justice and fairness, and satisfy the Northern mind and the requirements of the Government."[7]

In late June 1866, voters ratified the constitution and elected a conservative government headed by James W. Throckmorton, the Unionist who presided over the constitutional convention. The legislature refused to ratify the Thirteenth or Fourteenth Amendment, enacted "black codes" aimed at keeping freedmen in a status similar to slavery, and tried to send prominent secessionists to the U.S. Senate. Many Texas Unionists—and certainly Radical Republicans in Washington, D.C.—saw these actions as unrepentant and protested the new state constitution. Similar actions by state constitutional conventions across the South led Congress to move to control the Reconstruction process.

The Reconstruction Acts of 1867, which gave the U.S. Army responsibility for overseeing the process of Reconstruction in the South, also demanded that the former Confederate states adopt the Fourteenth Amendment. When Gen. Charles Griffin complained that Governor Throckmorton's attitudes and actions encouraged some of the violence that threatened Texas freedmen schools, Gen. Philip H. Sheridan approved the governor's removal. Elisha M. Pease became the new governor. Griffin began removing former Confederates from other state and local offices, and when he died, his replacement, Joseph J. Reynolds, continued the policy. Texas lawmakers also had to revise the constitution. The Texas Constitution of 1869 reflected the aims of the Radical Republicans.

## RISE AND FALL OF THE RADICAL
## REPUBLICAN SCHOOL SYSTEM

Among its provisions, the new state constitution established a centralized system of free public schools, structured the system under a state superintendent of education, set the school age for students at six to eighteen years, and provided a compulsory attendance law. The proceeds from the sale of public lands would fund the new school program, and the government would reestablish the permanent school fund with the income from property taxes, poll taxes, and other state revenues. The School Law of 1870, the enabling legislation of the new constitution's educational provisions, passed the following year. Like previous attempts at establishing a system of statewide public education, however, the effectiveness of the law was limited, for despite the apparent interest in education, and the Freedmen's Bureau and private schools that existed, the state started few public schools under the 1870 law.[8]

Much of the inertia was due to local resistance to the Republican school plan. From its inception, the new public school system contained many provisions that upset Reconstruction-era Texans. Many considered the office of state superintendent an unwelcome assertion of governmental power. Although the school term was only four months per year, the compulsory attendance laws not only affected the agricultural labor force, but it also undermined family authority in a time many considered education a parental prerogative. Many rural Texas families who depended upon their children to work in the fields saw the scholastic age range—six to eighteen years—as simply too broad. These years included children's most productive years, and the fact that for many rural families farmwork was a matter of survival, while education was considered a luxury, is reflected in the state literacy rates. In 1870, the National Bureau of Education reported that illiteracy rates for Texans above the age of ten stood at 17 percent for whites and 90 percent for African Americans. These numbers also reflect the common belief among white southerners that education was not important for African Americans. Although Texas placed no restrictions on educating slaves, most schooling was informal and utilitarian; it simply was not a common practice—and against the law in other southern states. The high illiteracy rate for African Americans immediately following the end of the Civil War reflects that reality. The resentment against efforts to formally educate freedmen following the war is evident in the numerous reports of violence and threats of violence against Freedmen's Bureau schools, teachers, and students and their families.[9]

Texas' efforts to build a statewide educational infrastructure coincided with other efforts influencing southern states to do likewise. In 1867, a northern philanthropist, George Peabody, established a fund to help former Confederate states create public school systems. In 1870, the Peabody Fund agent toured the state and "found the school laws and sentiment unsatisfactory" and led the Peabody board of trustees to decide not to allocate monies to Texas because the state lacked an educational organization. To address this issue, the School Law of 1871 ordered a state board of education to promote public schools, examine and appoint school teachers, fix teachers' salaries, define the course of study in public schools, select textbooks, and prescribe the duties of school districts' boards of directors. Texas governor Edmund J. Davis appointed former Union cavalry commander Jacob Carl DeGress to the position of state superintendent.[10]

DeGress had emigrated with his parents from Cologne, Prussia, in 1853. The family settled in Cape Girardeau, Missouri. He was nineteen in 1861 when he became the captain of a company of other German volunteers supporting the Union. His service was honored with several brevets. In 1864, he became Gen. Joseph A. Mower's aide-de-camp, and after the war came to Galveston with Mower and Gen. Gordon Grainger. He served in various military positions in Texas, most significantly as assistant commissioner of the Freedmen's Bureau in Houston. On January 1, 1867, he married Bettie Buckner, the widow of a Confederate officer and a cousin of future Houston mayor Joseph R. Morris's wife. He later accepted a commission in the regular army and was stationed at Fort Duncan in Eagle Pass as captain of Company L of the Ninth U.S. Cavalry, a Buffalo Soldier regiment assigned to protect West Texas from Indian depredations and border incursions. In December 1870, he resigned his commission because of the injuries he received at the siege of Vicksburg during the war. In May 1871, DeGress accepted an appointment to the superintendent's position, where he served through February 1874 when Radical Republican governor E. J. Davis was forced to surrender his office.[11]

DeGress faced opposition to the Republican school system from the outset. In September 1871, conservative opponents convened a taxpayers' convention to protest Governor Davis's administration. An organization composed of moderates and conservatives, the convention castigated the Davis administration for actions it considered "obnoxious," including the taxation provision of the School Law of 1871 because it gave free rein to the state government's painfully increasing "the taxes demanded of the people, and gaining the possession and control of enormous sums of money, the distribution whereof is subject to [the governor's] will, in connection with those about him, who hold position by his appointment, and whose terms of office depend on his pleasure."[12]

Critics also railed against the compulsory attendance policy because it took children away from the fields when they were most needed. Moreover, some cringed at the prospect of sending their children to schools run by Republican teachers. These concerns, as well as the perceived extravagances of the system, and distrust of the autocratic powers of the superintendent and state Board of Education, all fixed the minds of many Texans against the Republican school program. At the next election, the Republicans lost power in the state legislature to more conservative elements. The so-called Redeemers abolished the Radical Republican school system by the Constitution of 1876, although it had effectively ended in 1873. Despite its short life, the Radical Republican school program did realize some benefits. In the 1872–1873 school year, enrollment reached its apex, with approximately 125,000 students in public schools. The Radical system established the first free public schools in the state and expanded education for African Americans, which at the same time was a mark of its success and a cause for opposition. The number of public schools gives some account of the success of the program, compared with other furtive attempts at establishing a school system within the state.[13]

In the Constitution of 1876, Redeemer Democrats eliminated the office of state superintendent, compulsory attendance laws, and local taxation. The scholastic age was limited to eight to fourteen years. The constitution set a maximum of one quarter of the general revenue to be used for schools, but did not specifically require the legislature to set that amount aside. The School Law of 1876 implemented the constitution and established a state board of education with only minimal oversight. The "community school" system began under these laws. Under its provisions, parents in rural areas could petition the county judge to authorize an annually renewable school. The transitory nature of the community school system led to several perceived problems. Most schools operated for only a few months each year, school boards built no permanent buildings, and the requirement for yearly renewal caused local political strife. The state spent most of its funding for education on small, irregular schools, and there was no standardized curriculum or provisions for instructional continuity between schools. It was not long before the limitations of the decentralized plan became apparent. Influences from within and without the state contributed to a renewed interest in a more centralized school organization.[14]

## CONCERN OVER FUNDING INEQUALITY

In 1877, the Peabody Fund reconsidered its earlier decision to stop providing Texas schools educational funds. Dr. Barnas Sears of the Peabody board of directors addressed the Texas legislature and visited several cities advocating education, promoted establishing normal schools in the state, and encouraged increased teacher training. Baylor University president Dr. Rufus Burleson became the state Peabody agent and traveled the state encouraging free public education, including better-educated teachers, more supervision from the state Board of Education, and permanent school districts in Texas. In 1879, Texas governor Oran M. Roberts vetoed the school appropriation bill that set aside 25 percent of the state's general revenue for schools to force the legislature to cut spending. As a result, lawmakers cut back the state's education appropriation to one sixth of the state revenue, and they threatened to reduce teachers' salaries by stipulating that instructors had to maintain at least 75 percent classroom attendance to receive their salary. Roberts hoped that increased sale of public lands would make up for the cuts in state funding to schools, and he signed a law to sell public lands for fifty cents an acre. In the end, however, the public lands did not sell as well as Roberts planned, so although the state had reserved 52 million acres of land for public education, the amount generated from sales was minimal. Furthermore, ranchers and land speculators were the primary purchasers, so there were few improvements and local tax revenues remained low. As a result of the fiscal conservativism in Roberts's plan, enrollment in the public schools declined even though the state's population continued to grow.[15]

Following the austere financial situation of the Roberts administration, modifications in the educational system revealed that changes in public attitudes regarding the importance of funding public education emerged in the late nineteenth century. In 1880, former State Superintendent Orlando N. Hollingsworth began publishing the *Texas Journal of Education,* subsidized in part though Peabody education funds. The periodical promoted free public schools and other education reforms—especially, increased professional development and better training for public school teachers. Texas voters, reflecting a growing awareness of the need to provide additional financial support to public education, authorized a constitutional amendment in 1883 creating a district school system and local taxation. The next year, the legislature passed the School Law of 1884 that enabled the provisions of the constitutional amendment and also reestablished the office of state superintendent to supervise the school system. The law also called for a state tax and for investment of the School Fund into local school boards. The new laws provided more funds for city schools but not for the rural schools.[16]

From the mid-1880s through the early twentieth century, Texas classified public school districts either as independent or common, and the differences between the quality of teaching in independent and common schools became increasingly apparent. Independent school districts were located in towns and cities, which could maintain a population large enough to provide enough children to fill the schools. These schools operated on a more permanent basis than in rural areas, and because the children were not always engaged in farmwork, the schools operated longer than their rural counterparts. In the country, a school existed based on the number of children in the area. Local groups could more effectively control who went to school in rural areas. For example, school districts in East Texas and the Rio Grande Valley, where

African American and Mexican American children were concentrated, respectively, did not organize as many schools, and the 1884 law exempted more than fifty counties in these areas from organizing independent school districts to allow for local agricultural labor needs.

Southern historian C. Vann Woodward summed up the status of education in the early twentieth-century South as "miserably supported, poorly attended, wretchedly taught, and wholly inadequate for the education of the people." While the South suffered in comparison to the North in nearly all respects, Woodward continued, southern school systems were the least developed of all institutions in the region, and Texas was no exception. The average per diem expenditure per child in the South varied from as little as four cents for each Alabama child to ten cents for each Texas child.[17]

Across the nation in 1901, public schools spent an average per child of $21.14. Across the South, because of the dual system mandated by segregation, public schools averaged much less per child—$4.92 per white student and $2.21 for each African American student. Alabama spent an average of $3.10 per child, while North Carolina and South Carolina spent about $4.50, and Texas spent almost $6.60.[18]

Despite the fact that Texas spent more per child per diem than other southern states, it still ranked thirty-eighth in the nation in the number of children enrolled in school, thirty-seventh in per capita expenditures for education, and thirty-fifth in literacy. As this information became public, the state educational system received the blame for the state's poor quality of education. School reformers blamed the restrictions that Redeemer Democrats had placed upon school funding in the state constitution.[19]

## DISCREPANCIES BETWEEN URBAN AND RURAL SCHOOLS

The constitution put different limits on the amount of assessed property tax allowed in urban and rural areas. Urban areas could tax as much as fifty cents per one hundred dollar valuation, while rural areas were limited to only twenty cents. Rural schools could not issue building bonds, while independent districts in urban areas could. School-year length, or terms, also favored city schools, which could allow nine or more months per term; rural schools, however, had no mandatory term limits. In practice, by 1900 the average school term in city schools stood at 162 days, compared to 98 days for rural schools. This disparity also appears evident for state funds earmarked for rural areas. While urban school districts spent on average over eight dollars per pupil and rural schools spent only about five dollars, the number of school-age children enrolled in rural schools was more than three and a half times that entered in independent districts. Reformers saw the existing program as a political reaction against the earlier and more comprehensive Republican school program. They especially focused on what they considered the outdated rural "common schools."[20]

In their attempt to eliminate the Radical form of government, the Redeemers had destroyed a forward-looking school system, which would have served Texas children well, in exchange for a problem-wrought, ineffective, and reactionary system. "Restrictions were consciously and intentionally imposed against the free development of rural education," Frederick Eby wrote in 1925. "It is well-nigh incredible," Eby complained, "that such gross inequalities" were allowed to exist in a democratic society. It seemed even "more astonishing" that these "discriminations" against rural school children "were not accidental," but "had their foundations in the laws and constitutions of the state."[21]

Despite the larger number of children in rural areas, most rural teachers' salaries did not reflect the added responsibilities. Teachers in rural areas received only about half the pay of teachers in towns and cities. Perhaps fewer professionally trained teachers wanted to endure the limited resources of rural schools and sought employment in the independent districts, leaving the rural districts with fewer, if any, trained teachers. Only about 8 percent of rural schools (930 of 11,460) had reached enrollment sufficient enough to assign the students to different grades, the rest remained in "one-teacher, un-graded schools." Because the valuation of school property in cities also far exceeded the value in rural areas, the urban schools could afford to pay their teachers more than common schools.[22]

Educational-reform groups believed southern education remained wholly inadequate. Texas reformers, influenced by the Progressive movement, not only wanted to improve the state's educational system but also to eliminate the chasm separating the quality of education for rural Texas children from those who lived in towns and cities. Reformers traced the pattern of neglect from the Redeemer's reaction to the Radical Republicans' school system in the 1870s.

Migration from the rural to the urban areas accounts for one reason for the vast differences between city and rural schools. Problems facing farmers in the late nineteenth and early twentieth century, as well as a changing economy, convinced some people that greater economic opportunities awaited them away from the farms. If rural communities dwindled, common schools lost students and funds, and faced closure. Urban schools might have also benefited from greater attention than rural schools because reformers were concentrated in urban areas. At any event, while urban schools progressed, the rural schools languished. Nevertheless, nearly a quarter of a century passed before reformers turned their attention to the undeveloped parts of the countryside.

These contrasting 1907 photographs from the East Texas community of Diboll illustrate some of the challenges facing rural school teachers at the beginning of the 20th century. African American students are pictured with their teacher, J. W. Hogg. Although the segregated black school averaged forty students in attendance on a daily basis, it appears to be newer than the larger three-room white school. Daily attendance at the school for white children averaged 150 students, taught by W. A. O'Quinn, W. A. Wofford, and Mrs. Robert Kirby. The school for white children was much larger, and also featured glass window panes. Photographs courtesy The History Center, Diboll, Texas.

*Chapter 2*

# PROGRESSIVE REFORM
# IN TEXAS SCHOOLS

In the early 1900s, even in the tiny Fisher County community of Hobbs in West Texas, residents could boast, "Times were progressive." After a period of drought, migration into the Hobbs area increased. Established and new residents sought to increase the capacity of small rural schools by consolidation. One resident remembered:

> J. W. Hale, the county superintendent, envisioned a school in the rural area like the city school. These small schools only went to the seventh or eighth grade. If you wanted to go to high school you had to go into town. The men got together with Mr. Hale to build an eleven-year high school in this area. There was a large number of students in the area. An election was called, but prior to that, they had to have an act of the state legislature in order to create the consolidated where they could assess and collect taxes. The district would be independent.[1]

Another former student spoke of how the rural schools in the early 1900s adapted themselves to the agricultural cycle of the area:

> School was about six months long then. They would usually wait until the cotton was out to start school. The trustees would get together and check with the people around to see when they [the children] would be through picking cotton. Then they would start going to school. It was very much local control. They settled on the teacher's salary according to how much money they had. The teacher could take the job or not.[2]

One- and two-teacher rural schools also had to contend with students on a variety of scholastic levels, a situation that often meant that a teacher had to make the most expedient decisions, including overlooking students more advanced or those further behind:

At Riverdale, I had been accelerated in school, so they put me in the sixth grade when we started to school over at Perkel. That almost ruined me for being studious. There was nobody else in the sixth grade. When a teacher just has one pupil in a grade, it's very easy to pass him by and work with the ones that need working with. I sat there and daydreamed a good deal of the time. Instead of letting me go on and read my own history and let me write answers like teachers would do now, I just had to wait. I had United States history again because it was easier for me to have it with the other class than for the teacher to hear my lessons. So I skipped Texas history in grade school.[3]

## PROGRESSIVES AND SOUTHERN EDUCATION

Historians have named the first two decades of the twentieth century the Progressive Era, and they have labeled the impulse for political and social reform the Progressive movement. The Progressive epoch came in the wake of an economic upswing that followed the depression of 1893–97. The Progressive impulse spread across the nation so pervasively that by 1910 Progressives in the Republican Party, Democratic Party, and a third party they had formed combined to take control of the U.S. Congress. Yet the Progressive movement, unlike the earlier rural reform movements of the Farmers Alliances, the Grange, and the Populists, did not spring from one part of the nation; it achieved as much prominence in the South as in the North and had similar goals in both regions.[4]

Although a national movement, progressivism was not monolithic; it was supported by a wave of reform ideology that swept across the basic institutions of U.S. life and brought together a coalition of diverse interests. The movement combined Populist reformers, the proponents of Social Darwinism, the growing number of social scientists, and an educated and politically active middle class that worried that Victorian values were eroding in the rapidly changing and consumer-oriented society. While Progressives did not adapt the radicalism of the Agrarian movement, they did adopt a similar goal to reform the system from within in order "to ensure the survival of democracy" by building a government strong enough to offset the power of private industry. Like their Populist forerunners, Progressives tended to believe large industrial interests had grown powerful enough to threaten "the nation's institutions and life" in the late nineteenth and early twentieth century.[5]

Many southern Progressives advocated the importance of industrialization in diversifying the region's economy. An earlier generation of reformers, advocates of a "New South," had encouraged the benefits of industry as a means of building the region's wealth and economic infrastructure following the Civil War. The New South philosophy influenced the southern Progressives at the turn of the century and indeed blended with Populism in order to form a rural southern Progressivism that differed from urban southern Progressivism.[6]

The New South proponents had also emphasized the importance of improving the region's public schools. They advocated that a better-educated workforce would attract industry to the region. Jabez L. M. Curry, a secessionist and Confederate Congress representative, and briefly lieutenant in the Fifth Alabama Cavalry, was the best-known New South supporter of public school improvements. He became a Baptist minister after the Civil War, was an agent of the George Peabody Fund and the John Slater Fund, and recommended state normal schools, free public education, and graded schools. Booker T. Washington even acknowledged Curry's efforts to improve education for southern African Americans. Despite the efforts of reformers like Curry, the New South still ranked education reform below industrialization and agricultural reorganization in importance to the region's economic development.[7]

Southern Progressives shared the common Progressive goal of continuing "economic development and material progress," while at the same time developing a "more orderly and cohesive society." Some southern Progressives not only expressed concern with promoting stability in society, but they also possessed a genuine humanistic concern for those less fortunate than themselves. They felt a sense of responsibility for the ordinary citizens of the South who did not share their middle-class, professional heritage.[8]

In 1911, University of North Carolina English professor Edwin Mims wrote that scientific advancement and "social well being" would benefit people throughout the region. Money from northern philanthropists was solicited and distributed across the South to help alleviate the social ills that had plagued the region. Reformers included poverty, ignorance, disease, parasites, and racial problems among the list of problems affecting the South.[9]

Progressives realized that these were the same issues the Radical Republicans, Redeemer Democrats, and Populists had sought to address, but southern Progressives had an advantage over their predecessors. The issues were no longer solely regional; instead, they became part of a great national movement. Progressives across the nation welcomed "innovations and reforms" politically, economically, and socially. They wanted intelligent discussions of social problems and "skilled leadership" to overcome them.[10]

The apex of the Texas Progressive movement came with the election of Woodrow Wilson in the 1912 elections. Reform-minded Texans had admired Wilson from the time he won the gubernatorial election in New Jersey in 1910. Southern Progressives also emerged victorious in the congressional elections the same year Wilson was elected president. The Sixty-third Congress became the first Congress controlled by southern Democrats since before the Civil War. Representatives from the eleven former Confederate states controlled twenty-two committees, and the Texas delegation was the largest from the South.[11]

Disillusionment over Wilson's failure at Versailles and his inability to persuade Congress to accept League of Nations membership, however, led to the decline of the national Progressive movement. The coalition that supported Wilson in 1912 and reelected him in 1916 fell apart in the wake of the World War I. Despite the loss of political power after the war, the Progressive spirit continued throughout the 1920s. As support for Wilson declined, the diverse elements that had formed the Democratic coalition—farmers, organized labor, urban Democratic organizations, public works developers, social workers, and other independent organizations—retained elements of their Progressive natures, even when unable to occupy common ground. The perpetuation of the Progressive impulse by these various interest groups is important to the study of southern politics and reform in the first two decades of the twentieth century. Although the reform impulse evolved because of changing attitudes as well as local and regional factors, the Progressive spirit remained. This is especially true where educational reform was concerned, as attention to improving southern education steadily increased even after enthusiasm for other Progressive reform objectives had declined.[12]

Across the region, except for Mississippi, Florida, and Alabama, most southern states devoted over 70 percent of their budgets for the development of good roads, the promotion of industry, and educational improvements. This represented a dramatic change in southern attitude toward public education. While education in the South was once considered secondary by some, or even unimportant, by the early twentieth century education and professional training became an economic necessity.

One contemporary journalist claimed the threat to the region's agricultural economy by the "boil weevil and the sudden awakening to the errors of the past" caused southerners "to turn with almost pathetic yearning to men of authority." While the call for better public education had been sounded at various times across the South, Progressives and professionals finally gave educational reform the support it needed.[13]

The southern Progressives sought educational reform for schools in the burgeoning towns and cities of New South. Many young people from the country left the family farms for southern urban areas that held out to them the promise of increasing opportunities. Southern businessmen also began to heed the warnings that "unintelligent, unskillful labor" was not only "unprofitable, but dangerous." Illiteracy remained widespread among the labor force in the South. Although traditional southern education favored white males, nearly 20 percent of them could neither read nor write. The 50 percent illiteracy rate of the African American population also reflected the poor educational opportunities afforded them by the Jim Crow segregation policies and a lack of money allocated to educating African Americans in the South, especially in rural areas.[14] W. H. Heck wrote in 1904:

> During this time, the rural districts were sadly neglected. The people followed their fathers in the routine of farming, with little desire to . . . improve their material and intellectual status. Most of the school officials performed their duties perfunctorily, and the people naturally came to regard the district-school in its barnlike building, with its poorly prepared teacher and its three or four months' tasting of textbooks unrelated to the children's lives, as a thing of little public or personal interest.[15]

Public education in the southern urban and industrial areas, therefore, served to train a better, more efficient, and more productive labor force. The emerging southern African American middle class and educational reformers were also advocating improved schools and educational opportunities for black students. African American leaders urged self-help programs and Progressive ideology to seek out concessions from whites interested in helping hardworking, "New South" African Americans.[16]

Progressives also saw the need for improved rural education as well. Many feared that the siren song of the cities, which lured many young southerners away from the family farm, threatened to become the swan song for the rural South. Across the South, urbanization caused rural communities to suffer. Rural ministers saw significant reductions in their congregations and collection plate revenues—and salaries—as parishioners migrated away to towns and cities. Rural school enrollments fell as families left the farm, so districts were forced to increase their size to accommodate the students who remained, making transportation more difficult as students had to travel farther. Moreover, fewer families meant less support for rural schools, leading to less money for rural teachers' salaries and making rural school assignments less attractive for qualified teachers, thus leading to a lack of certified teachers in rural schools. It was a vicious cycle of cause and effect for rural schools, which in turn led more families to look toward educating their children at the better schools in town.[17] In 1915, the president of the Texas Farmers' Congress, H. E. Singleton, mourned the erosion of rural population:

> The country man is fast recognizing that the towns are drawing the best and strongest character from the country to the town. And the towns have noted an increase in their population of retired farmers. The country has lost much, and the towns gain but little by the change.[18]

## THE COUNTRY LIFE MOVEMENT AND PUBLIC SCHOOLS

The Country Life Movement, a back-to-the-farm philosophy, was popular among Progressives beginning in the early twentieth century. In 1907, President Theodore Roosevelt convened a Country Life Commission to study rural problems. Improving rural schools was one of the solutions commissioners recommended.[19] Teaching youngsters how to grow crops scientifically might slow the migration to the urban areas. Education no longer seemed a luxury; it was a necessity. "Every man who, without the aid of liberal education, has made what the world calls a 'practical success' out of farm operations," Singleton observed, "realizes how much an education would have helped."[20]

Frederick T. Gates of the General Education Board (established in 1902 to disburse funds given by John D. Rockefeller) advocated a comprehensive Progressive curriculum for rural schools. He advocated a "healthful, intelligent, efficient" country life, where rural schools, with the help of experts from agricultural colleges, forestry, and veterinarians, would take on the problems plaguing farm society and boldly predicted "they shall solve them."[21] Gates believed serious educational reforms in rural southern schools were imperative:

> We call to mind that, for a century past, one *Titanic,* at least, full of children, with some adults, has gone down every month in the South, for lack of knowledge of a few simple facts about the hygiene of rural homes and their surroundings, and for a lack of proper clothing for the feet of the children.[22]

Noting the curriculum reform occurring in northern urban schools, Gates observed that these reforms could also benefit students enrolled in rural schools. A proper rural school curriculum would not stifle children's instincts

but would guide them to their "natural aspirations." He proposed that studying the natural environment should be just as important in the new country
school program as the "three R's," which would be taught for their practical
purposes, not to some "abstract end." Once teachers presented the practical
application of the essentials, children would "learn to use them easily and
naturally." Gates believed, as did other Progressive education advocates, that
an important function of education was to teach children how to interact
with others socially, with "courtesy, helpfulness, gentleness, deference, truth,
reverence, honor, [and] chivalry." As historian David Tyack described it, education leaders wanted professionals to design a standard, "one best system" to
instill community values and trade skills.[23]

In order to accomplish this, Progressives sought to expand educational
opportunities to reach all children. Universal education became a fundamental tenant in the Progressive ideology of extending democracy. Additionally,
southerners saw education as a means of improving the region's labor force
and industrial technology. Reformers also realized the possibility that school
reform would expand beyond the classroom to influence family and community life. Through health instruction and vocational education training,
schools could adapt their curriculum to meet the individual needs of the student and the community. In the end, such education would extend culture
to the masses and result in general social improvement.[24]

Rural Progressive school reformers in Texas, and across the South, thus
saw education as a catalyst for social reform. Education consequently attracted northern philanthropists, served as a "redemptive force" in the South,
allowed for cooperation between North and South, and affected the lives of
more southerners than any other social reform. This proved especially true in
rural areas as the primary focus of educational reform in the South became
rural schools.[25]

## LEGISLATING SCHOOL REFORM

Across the South and in Texas, Progressives sought to convince the public
to join their efforts in "an attempt to develop the moral will, the intellectual
insight, and the political and administrative agencies" necessary to advance
their causes. In the crusade to improve the region's public schools, reformers
struggled to persuade southern citizens of the need for educational reform. In
some cases, this took on an almost revival-like atmosphere.[26]

In February 1907, a group of concerned educators, laymen, and state officials met in Austin to discuss solutions to reform the educational system. The
group met at the behest of Dr. William Seneca Sutton, professor of education
at the University of Texas, who had earlier published an article comparing
Texas schools to those in other states. The meeting evolved into an annual
Conference for Education in Texas, presided over by Clarence W. Ousley,
editor of the *Fort Worth Record,* who also served as chair of the Conference's
executive board. The Conference met yearly for only five years, yet although
short-lived it achieved considerable success in convincing the public of the
importance of improved schools in Texas.[27]

In 1908, the Conference joined with other professional organizations, including the state Board of Medical Examiners, the Texas Farmers' Congress,
the state Democratic Convention, the presidents of six leading denomina-
tional colleges, and the Texas Federation of Women's Clubs in successfully
campaigning for three amendments to improve public school funding. The
next year the Conference supported legislation to form school districts and
encourage consolidation of rural schools. Other laws over the next few years
abolished the community school system, which had been in place since the
School Law of 1876.[28]

Progressives also spearheaded other attempts to bring rural schools up to
par with those in the cities. In 1907, the legislature mandated that all textbooks had to be adopted for a minimum of five years. The legislature then
allowed districts to assign these texts to students, who could then purchase
the texts from teachers. Beginning in 1919, the state provided free textbooks.
Districts could adopt multiple lists of texts under a 1925 law to compensate
for the problems the state had with delays in delivery by some publishers. By
1929, the state Board of Education received the power to adopt textbooks.[29]

Other significant Progressive changes occurred in Texas education. In
1911, legislators established the Normal School Board of Regents to oversee
teacher training. The Rural High School Law the same year created county
boards of education that classified rural schools and prescribed their curriculum, established new rural high schools, consolidated common school
districts, and ensured that rural high schools were teaching the same courses
as city high schools. The law also budgeted fifty thousand dollars to provide
a two thousand dollar matching grant for any school district to establish
agricultural, home economics, and vocational training classes. In 1917, the
legislature established the state Department of Education to assume the duties of enforcing the Rural High School Law. The state Board of Education

replaced the Department of Education in 1929 to oversee apportionment, distribution, and investment of the state public school funds and textbook selection.[30]

Attendance among rural school children remained a problem. In Texas, primarily an agricultural state, school-aged children in rural areas assisted their families in planting and harvesting crops. William A. Owens's *This Stubborn Soil* illustrates that in the early twentieth century education still ranked as a luxury that occupied a distant second place to making a living. Therefore, it is not surprising that a compulsory attendance bill failed to pass the legislature in 1905. Finally, after ten years, lawmakers required children aged eight to ten to attend classes for at least sixty days each school year. By 1917, students were required to attend school for one hundred days, and the school term increased to 156 days by 1929.[31]

Progressives and educational reformers focused their attention on amending the Texas Constitution to bring the country schools into parity with the independent school districts in incorporated towns. As evidence of the revival of interest in rural education that swept the state in the 1910s, the Democratic gubernatorial candidate James E. Ferguson included in his platform a pledge to improve the conditions of the rural schools. Once elected governor in 1914, Ferguson advocated a "Million Dollar Appropriation for Country Schools." The legislature allocated this amount over a two-year period, from September 1, 1915, to August 31, 1917. Over thirteen hundred schools in almost two hundred counties benefited from this allocation.[32]

## THE BETTER SCHOOLS CAMPAIGN

The "Better Schools Campaign" of 1919–20 ranked as the most obvious Progressive-led reform attempt. Annie Webb Blanton, the first woman to become president of the Texas State Teacher's Association (1916) and later state superintendent of public instruction (1919–1923), organized the campaign to persuade voters to approve a constitutional amendment that would repeal the fifty cents per hundred dollar ad valorem limit. This would allow local districts to increase taxation to maintain efficient schools. The economic problems that followed World War I had increased the difficulty the state had in financing its large share of school system costs. If the amendment passed, local funding would increase.[33]

The Better Schools Campaign became a grassroots movement with a massive distribution of literature, public speeches, songs, slogans, and press support. One flyer proclaimed the state was

> *First* in Size.
> *First* in Agricultural Products.
> *First* in Production of Cotton.
> *Third* in Production of Oil.
> *Seventh* in Wealth.
> *Thirty-Ninth* in Education.
>
> Shall Texas keep this rank?
>
> Work and vote for the Better Schools Amendment,
> November 2.[34]

The amendment passed by a margin of almost two to one.[35]

Curriculum modernization also took place in the 1920s as agricultural and vocational instruction and new social science courses were added. Boys learned business and industrial skills, while girls took home economics and secretarial courses. All children had recess period added to their class schedules, and schools employed nurses to provide health care for the students. Standardized testing became a diagnostic tool for administrators, and teachers began using lesson plans and incorporating audio-visual aids in their classes.

Junior high schools also developed during the Progressive Era. The junior schools, said Walter D. Cocking, director of junior education for San Antonio, were organized as preparatory schools for the high school curriculum. Junior high teachers would expose students to all subjects so that by the time the students entered senior high school, they would "have learned enough about all fields in general to know what [they want] to do and can do best."[36]

## THE EFFICIENCY MOVEMENT AND SCHOOL SURVEYS

Progressive educators also wanted to eliminate waste in the public school operations and drew inspiration from Fredrick Winslow Taylor's emphasis on efficiency in managerial practices. They applied the principles of "Taylorism" to public school administration, believing efficiency saved money and eliminated corruption. Between 1900 and 1925, efficiency in school administration and organization became a common theme among professional educational journals and publications, politicians, and the general public. Educational reformers also advocated that "more emphasis be placed upon a practical and immediately useful education"—a more utilitarian education—rather than a strictly academic curriculum that served only for personal enrichment.[37]

In order to measure the efficiency of schools under their supervision, school district boards commissioned professional surveys. The school survey became immensely popular, with almost two hundred completed between 1911 and 1930. Applying the principals of Taylor's scientific management to education, some surveys analyzed the number of minutes students spent learning spelling or questioned whether students who probably would not attend college should take courses like algebra. Educational historians David Tyack and Elisabeth Hansot have described school surveys as educational muckraking, permitting reformers to "expose evils, foundation officials to gain leverage to change society, and federal or state educational bureaucrats to enlarge governmental power to regulate or standardize." Texas lawmakers requested two professional school surveys, the first occurred in the 1920s, and another was conducted during the Depression. The results of the latter survey led to a call for a drastic overhaul to the state's school system.[38]

## W. LEE "PAPPY" O'DANIEL AND PUBLIC SCHOOL REFORM

At 8:30 A.M. Sunday morning, October 15, 1939, radio sets crackled across Texas with the sounds of *Home Sweet Home*. Then an announcer stated that the Texas governor would soon be speaking to listeners from the Governor's Mansion in Austin. In confirmation of the announcer's promise, the governor's "friendly voice" chimed in. "Good morning ladies and gentlemen, and hello there boys and girls, this is W. Lee O'Daniel speaking right direct from our 'front room' here in this beautiful Governor's Mansion." He explained that he had sent a letter to all members of the Texas legislature letting them know that he intended to call a special session to consider his social security plan. After noting that he had not yet received a reply from all legislators, he urged dawdlers to reply at once. The governor then turned his attention to "a problem which is close to the heart of every mother and father in Texas": the inequality of the Texas public school system.[39]

In 1939, most Texans were not shocked to hear that their public schools were unequal. And those who voted for O'Daniel were not surprised to hear the governor say he would be at the forefront of a movement to right this terrible wrong. He had campaigned, after all, on a platform consisting of the Ten Commandments, the Golden Rule, and an end to corrupt professional politicians. While these may seem hackneyed ideas compared to today's campaign rhetoric, to Texas voters in the 1930s these platitudes seemed reasonable solutions to help resolve the terrible economic crisis caused by the Great Depression and the Dust Bowl. Simplistic solutions to complex problems often have popular appeal, and the governor was not above pandering to the crowd.

Long regarded as a political opportunist and hack, Wilbert Lee "Pass-the-Biscuits-Pappy" O'Daniel's gubernatorial administration has been described as at best unproductive, and at worst a "vaudevillian atmosphere" characterized by "medicine show tactics." Many of his plans and proposals came under fire. For example, his major gubernatorial campaign promise focused on an old-age pension that raised opposition from many sides because of the costs associated with such a program, especially during a time of economic hardship. His opposition to the death penalty also raised many eyebrows. O'Daniel was warned in late 1938 that "any attempt by the governor-elect, or by any other agency of the state, to tamper with the death penalty will be vigorously opposed." President of the District and County Attorneys Association of Texas, Dallas District Attorney Andrew Patton, feared that elimination of capital punishment in the state would lead to statewide chaos, "lynchings, mob violence, and an outbreak of murder that would shock the nation." Indeed, one student of Texas political history stated, "controversy seemed to swirl whenever he opened his mouth."[40]

Even more frustrating, the governor's conviction for his own program seemed lacking. Early in January 1939, at the beginning of his first term, O'Daniel promised that he would not fight the legislature in favor of bills he supported. "If you read in the newspapers, while the legislature is in session," he stated, "that the governor is engaged in a great battle with the legislature over the passage of a certain bill, you may know that it is not true." He explained, "I have no constitutional authority to battle with them and do not intend to do so." Instead, the people who elected the state representatives and senators could influence their elected officials while he as governor could keep the public informed of legislation that he thought important.[41]

Keeping the public informed proved to be the governor's forte, while his interaction with the Texas legislature and the diverse state boards and agencies left much to be expected. O'Daniel promised voters an increase in the pension for elderly Texans during his initial campaign, an especially important issue during the Depression. The proposed increase never materialized because neither the legislature nor the governor could decide upon a way to pay for the promised relief without raising taxes, which has never been a politically popular option. The governor spent most of his first two-year term railing against the "professional politicians" in Austin, and the "entrenched oligarchies"—meaning state agencies who refused to cooperate with his programs and promises—as the reasons for his political ineffectiveness. His weekly radio broadcasts, which he had originally started as advertising for his flour mill long before he ran for governor, continued throughout his term in office. He used the programs as a way of communicating with his constituency, denouncing political opponents, and delivering homespun homilies advocating the Golden Rule and the Ten Commandments.

He won his second term, despite his failure to secure most of the promises of his first campaign, when a record number of Texas voters returned O'Daniel to the governor's mansion. Lady Bird Johnson said of O'Daniel's political juggernaut, "You couldn't find anybody who voted for him, but he always won the election." To be sure, the governor garnered over 54 percent of the almost 1.19 million votes cast in the 1940 election. The reason for his popularity seemed to stem from older, farm residents. Indeed, his approval rating among farmers in the fall of 1940 measured almost 78 percent, over 71 percent among rural Texans, and more than 74 percent among voters over the age of fifty. Economically, his constituency seemed to be those Texans with the lowest income. Thus, it appears that the governor championed those hit hardest by the economic downturn of the 1930s: older, rural, lower-income Texans. They believed the governor's explanations that "professional politicians" stymied his agenda and appreciated his personal weekly radio broadcasts. This would account for one man's explanation of his vote for O'Daniel: "He's a good man; it ain't his fault he didn't do nothing."[42]

Former Speaker Claud Gilmer remembered the rural grassroots popularity of O'Daniel's campaign:

> I didn't really pay much attention to it. You know, I had been listening to these Light Crust Dough Boys and what have you. I went into this little grocery store in Menard. This is while I was making my rounds running for the House, and this was out where about three or four country roads come into town. There is this little grocery store, you know, and [the owners would] buy their eggs and sell them things. I said something to him about O'Daniel. I said, "He keeps talking about all these petitions that he gets and so forth and so on." I said, "You reckon that's for real?" He said, "You better believe it." He took me over there

and showed me. He said, "Everybody that trades in here is signing these things and sending them to him." From then on I believed the O'Daniel story.[43]

Yet the very rural nature of O'Daniel's supporters doomed the governor's proposal to restructure the state's public education system and public schools in general.

Governor O'Daniel noted in his mid-October radio broadcast that the state had commissioned a survey about the public schools in 1925. The report, he claimed, "pointed out . . . that the public school system in Texas was costing too much in proportion to the benefits received from it and that one of the changes urgently needed was a reorganization to cut administrative districts and administrative costs." The Works Project Administration funded another school survey in 1938.[44] "It is a wonderful report," he promised, "but friends, this 1800-page report resting on the shelves of the various libraries, regardless of how much information it contains, will serve no useful purpose." While both surveys made good recommendations, O'Daniel could see no meaningful changes in the school system that resulted from the surveys. If a business manager spent "five or six hundred thousand dollars to make a market survey and then simply file the survey and never use it," O'Daniel cautioned, he "would probably not be looked upon by his associates as a very competent associate."[45]

O'Daniel summed up some of the findings of the 1938 report. Out of Texas' almost 6,800 school districts, independent districts numbered just over one thousand. The other 5,700 were common school districts. Of the almost fifty thousand public school teachers in the state, 10 percent worked in small schools, with three or fewer teachers.[46]

The governor revealed to listeners the vast amount of money the state spent on public education. The state's public schools cost taxpayers about $85 million annually. Sixty-five million dollars of that amount went to pay the salaries of teachers and support staff. The state allocated $22 per child to the school districts. The governor estimated that amount at $34 million based upon 1.56 million scholastics. Texas also furnished textbooks at a cost of almost two million dollars each year. The legislature allocated another seven million dollars for Rural Aid, monies paid to rural districts without high schools to provide transportation and tuition for students who wanted to attend a nearby high school, and to districts unable to meet the salaries of their teachers. Moreover, another million dollars went to provide for homemaking, agricultural and vocational training classes, and eleemosynary instruction for children with physical limitations. Another four hundred thousand dollars supported the activities of the state board of education. Thus, the governor pointed out, the people of Texas paid for $44.5 million, with the remaining $20.5 million of the above-mentioned $65 million generated from local taxation. Payments and interest on school bonds accounted for $20 million. All together, the state spent $85 million annually for public education.[47]

After the governor detailed the costs of Texas schools, he pointed out that inequalities existed within the system. Nearly 29,000 students attended one of 700 schools in the state that operated less than six months out of the year. Some 205,000 children attended one- or two- teacher schools. The most glaring inequalities in state education had to do with funding. Forty-four thousand Texas children attended 413 schools without any tax base. Another two thousand districts levied only the minimum ad valorem tax of fifty cents per one hundred dollar valuation. On the other hand, some districts profited from county-controlled lands where oil companies took out leases and paid royalties. Schools in poorer areas could not compete with the tax base of wealthier districts. In addition to this inequity, the amounts did not take into consideration a taxpayer's ability to pay when it apportioned school funds. Not only did the value of land vary across the state, because the amount of land varied in each county, the total revenue each county generated could differ anywhere from as little as $205 per student in poorer counties to as much as $18,000 per student in wealthier counties. This, said O'Daniel, "is one of the greatest inequalities that exists in our school system."[48]

O'Daniel pointed out that the differences in property valuation for each county contributed to unequal educational opportunity for Texas school-age children. The governor explained to his audience that while local control was important to schools in Texas, the state had an interest. The disparity in funding affected student-to-teacher ratios in classrooms and even the quality of teachers hired by districts. Poorer districts could not afford to hire better-trained, more experienced educators, the governor posited, but "must rely upon young, inexperienced teachers who have had the minimum of training allowed by the State in securing a license to teach."[49] The small districts with the one- and two-teacher schools simply could not provide the same education as larger schools. Governor O'Daniel explained: "These inequalities permit a portion of our boys and girls to have much better educational opportunities than others." He quickly assured his rural supporters that he did not advocate doing away with small, rural schools, but he did believe that the public wanted "good schools, run . . . as economically as they can be without sacrificing their efficiency." Moreover, another contributing factor to inefficiency and waste was the way the funds were distributed. The state

allocated funds based upon the number of school-age children in the counties. Attendance did not influence the amount of funding. Thus, a school in
an area with a high number of school-age children would receive more state
funding than areas with fewer children regardless of whether the children
attended the schools or not.[50]

O'Daniel appointed a committee of 168 educators and administrators
to study the problems in the school system and suggest legislation. The next
year, the committee presented its recommendations to the governor. They
included the creation of a state board of education led by an *appointed* superintendent, increased consolidation of smaller districts, teacher specialization,
trained administrators, a twelve-year school program, curriculum standardization, and the establishment of a guaranteed minimum program of instruction funded locally and by the state to fund schools at an amount equal to at
least $70 per student.[51]

## L. A. WOODS AND OPPOSITION TO PUBLIC SCHOOL CHANGE

Opposition to the recommendations arose soon after the committee released
its report. Littleton A. Woods, the elected state superintendent of public education, emerged as one of the most outspoken critics of the proposed reform.
While acknowledging the need for most of the recommendations, including
a standardized curriculum, better-trained teachers and administrators, and
a method of determining average daily attendance, he stubbornly disagreed
with what he considered a violation of the "fundamental principles of a
Democracy"—namely, an appointed state superintendent. O'Daniel's office
received many letters from citizens, administrators, and teachers criticizing
the recommendations. Like the superintendent, many opposed the idea of an
appointed—rather than elected—state superintendent. The three members
of the Cone School Board summarized much of the opposition when they
wrote to the governor, "We think this plan is undemocratic and will not be
to the interest of the rural schools and rural communities."[52]

Woods apparently encouraged opposition to the governor's plan in public speeches calling the idea of an appointed superintendent "bureaucratic."[53]
He even went so far as to suggest a constitutional amendment to extend the
term for the office of state superintendent of public instruction from a two-
year to a four-year elected position.[54] He suggested that the longer term
would allow for more school improvements. He also suggested that improve-

ments would come with increased funding. When reports released by the state Department of Education in early December 1940 ranked Texas schools twenty-fifth in the nation, by the end of the week Woods responded that with an additional $5 million Texas schools could have a first-class rating.[55] With opposition coming from rural constituents as well as the state superintendent's office, and a reelection bid looming, O'Daniel dropped the proposed changes to the state school system, but the renewal of interest in changing schools sparked a conflagration.

If O'Daniel quickly lost interest in restructuring the Texas public school system, his short-lived crusade set in motion a larger public debate on the issue. In 1940, W. L. Hughes, chair of Texas A&M's department of education, criticized the inefficiency in the school system, calling it "an archaic, horse-and-buggy form of school organization and administration." If educators themselves did not work together to create a more efficient school system, he warned, "our legislature will do as the legislatures in some other states have done, that is, take the problem in hand, and without asking us, set up a more economical, and more efficient form of school government." He argued that the state superintendent's office should not be an elected position and called for a more powerful state board of education. He also called for a consolidation of smaller school districts, better-trained teachers, a more equitable distribution of state educational funds, and curriculum improvements. "The school system of Texas was never planned," he asserted, "it has simply 'growed up.'" He suggested that educators themselves must spread the word that the system was obsolete and needed restructuring. "It is our job to educate the people," he stated, "it is our obligation to educate the people to think progressively and constructively in the matter of educating their children."[56]

Professor Hughes was a harbinger of the criticisms of the Texas public school system that came on the eve of World War II. Indeed, the 1940s saw a renewal of interest in creating a more efficient state school system with educators in the vanguard of the reform movement. They targeted the rural schools primarily. A survey of schools across the nation for the 1939–40 school year revealed that schools that could budget $3,000 per year for the average classroom were able to provide better quality instruction, as well as more diversity in curriculum. Schools that spent below the $3,000 mark tended to focus on rote memorization and classroom drill activities. Yet, the national average budget was $1,650 per classroom. The survey revealed that schools that could afford no more than $1,000 per classroom were "miserable schools generally employing poorly qualified and poorly paid teachers, who do uninspiring teaching in unattractive if not unhealthful classrooms, with few books and little or no instructional equipment." Early in 1941, the Texas State Teachers Association research department noted that smaller and rural districts with one-room schools could not support themselves through local taxation. Even more importantly "the poor quality of education afforded [rural] children presents the real cost."[57]

By the end of the Progressive Era, the critiques of the old public school system were becoming more pronounced. Yet Progressives faced tremendous opposition, deeply rooted in the attitudes and traditions of the people of Texas. Texans, Frederick Eby wrote, had deceived themselves about the effectiveness of their public schools because they allowed themselves to be "flattered by the boasts of office-seeking politicians" that Texas had the best schools and the "largest school fund of all." Progressive educators thus had to persuade the voters that "these notions" of the supremacy of Texas schools made "by provincial politicians were wholly erroneous." Most people, however, were not aware of the changes taking place in school systems in other states that, when compared with the Texas system, made schools in the Lone Star state seem backward in comparison. Most people had little awareness of national standards for educational achievement. Many Texans had themselves attended only the makeshift schools of the rural districts with limited access to progressive methods, so they could neither appreciate the spirit of reform nor the curricular and instructional changes advocated by educational reformers across the nation.[58]

Education, at the turn of the century, was considered "a redemptive force" in the betterment of the region because it had the opportunity affect the lives of more southerners than any other Progressive program. Progressives sought to turn the tide from ad hoc common schools and decentralized organization and breathe new life into the state's educational system, not to the benefit of white children alone, but to minority children as well. Cecil E. Evans, president of Southwest Texas State Teachers College (1911–1942), echoed the "Melting Pot" theory that a "cosmopolitan population makes us a stronger nation." He clearly stated, "They should have equal opportunities with all other Americans." Yet, while Progressive educators, like their New South predecessors, may have believed in educational equality for all races, in practice this was not the case. Educational opportunity for Mexican Americans and African Americans remained behind that of white children.[59]

As Governor O'Daniel's attempt to overhaul the public school system exemplified, despite their enthusiasm and campaigns for educational uplift, reformers needed the support of the public and their lawmakers. While surveys and reports could demonstrate the need for educational revision, without the legal and financial support of the legislature, school reformers could only rally public support for change. Social and political developments during the 1940s and World War II provided the impetus for change. Texans began to realize the benefits of improving public education for minority and white children in rural areas and, more importantly, they had the economic ability to do it.

Rae Files Still (center) poses with W. Lee and Merle O'Daniel in 1941. Still, who represented Waxahachie in the 47th through 51st Legislature, chaired the Education Committee, was a member of the Gilmer-Aikin committee and sponsored the legislation in the House. She detailed the history of the legislation in *The Gilmer-Aikin Bills: A Study in the Legislative Process* in 1950. Between legislative sessions, she taught public school. Photograph 1976/8-423 "Governor & Mrs. O'Daniel with Rae Files" courtesy Texas State Library and Archives Commission.

*Chapter 3*

# MINORITIES IN TEXAS
# SCHOOLS, 1920–1949

Although Progressive educational reformers worked to improve public school conditions across the state by focusing their energies on the outdated rural one-room schools, they often overlooked the conditions Texas minorities faced in classrooms. Ironically, most minority children in the state attended rural schools, African American children in East Texas and Mexican and Mexican American students in South Texas. Both groups faced limitations on their education. Many attended schools with conditions similar to those of poor white children who also worked and lived on farms in rural Texas. The cycle of poverty that demanded all family members work to bring in the crops competed with the desire to provide children with an education. Students went to school when and where they could, in schools of varying degrees of disrepair, taking a host of classes without a common curriculum, and managed by teachers with greatly varying qualifications.

If the vagaries and varieties of experience in rural schools hindered poor white students, segregation and a lack of funding compounded the lack of resources for African American and Mexican American students in Texas. Organizations like the National Association for the Advancement of Colored People (NAACP) and the League of United Latin American Citizens (LULAC) organized legal challenges to segregation in public schools beginning in the 1930s. This chapter will examine some of the hindrances Texas minorities experienced in public schools during the first half of the twentieth century. It will then track the evolving attitudes educators held about the proper role of education for minority students between the Progressive Era and World War II and discuss changes in segregation practices in schools on the eve of the *Brown* decision.

## EDUCATION FOR AFRICAN AMERICANS IN TEXAS

Historians have documented the struggle African Americans faced in providing their children an education. Although southern states maintained separate public education facilities, equal educational opportunity for African American school children "was a statutory myth." The balance sheet provides the primary evidence of the inequality in African Americans' education. Although Texas led the South with the highest literacy rate among African Americans, black schools still lagged behind their white counterparts in funds, faculty, and facilities. Texas and Oklahoma spent almost double on a white student what they did on a black student. Other southern states spent even less. South Carolina spent ten times the amount on educating whites as it did on African Americans.[1]

In July 1945, the *Dallas Morning News* commissioned Joseph J. Rhoads, president of Bishop College, to write an article commenting on the minimum educational needs for black Texans. He began by stating the meaninglessness of the question. "The incident of color and the social fact of race have no real significance in the formulation of programs of education," he wrote. In fact, he asserted, "the Texas Negro refuses to subscribe to the vicious theory that a special brand of education may be prescribed to meet the 'peculiar needs' of his race." He then emphasized the need for African American students to receive the best education possible. "It is preposterous then to assume," he asserted, that a black student in Texas "can meet the demands of a rapidly advancing democratic society with fewer opportunities for education than his fellow Americans require."[2]

The lack of funding for black schools resulted in higher illiteracy rates. At the end of the Reconstruction period, more than three-quarters of the African American population over age ten were illiterate. Although the rate of illiteracy declined over the years, by 1940 the problem still affected 10 to 15 percent of blacks in the South. During the same period, the illiteracy rate for whites over the age of ten dropped from 21 to 5 percent. Illiteracy combined with farm tenancy to create a self-perpetuating cycle of poverty that most African Americans in the South could not escape.[3]

Even if Texas blacks did not languish from illiteracy, there may not have been books for them to read. In 1924, an overwhelming majority of black schools in Texas did not have a librarian; most, in fact, were one-teacher schools. The lack of librarians may explain why, by 1940, there were fewer books in Texas' African American schools than the total number of black students. "Money spent on the education of Negroes was a waste" appeared to be the prevailing attitude held by many whites in the first half of the twentieth century. One African American teacher in Texas remembered her first assignment to a rough-hewn, unpainted, rural one-room school near Hallettsville. The facility lacked playground equipment, landscaping, and a water supply. "There was a rusty wood-burning heater but no wood," she wrote. A few years later, at another school, she noted a "grave disparity between the state allocation and the actual expenditures" at the school. When she brought this to the attention of a trustee, he angrily asked her if she was accusing someone on the board of misappropriating funds. East Texas senator James Taylor charged that school districts would "count all the black kids in order to get the money." However, once the funds were allocated, "they didn't even care if the [children] went to the school or not."[4]

Texas provided little money to black schools and restricted the tax rates in areas where African Americans were concentrated, thus local school taxes that could have been used to benefit African American schools were low. The School Law of 1884 was designed to establish permanent rural independent school districts and provide for local taxation to support rural districts, but it exempted those counties with the heaviest concentration of African American students. Faced with the lack of public funds, black schools were forced to depend upon the private contributions of students' parents, who donated money as well as their time and skills, and sometimes buildings. African American adults leased their barns and other empty buildings, or assisted in cleaning up and making repairs on existing schools. Several private charitable foundations also offered monies to provide for African American education in Texas and throughout the South, including the General Education Board, the Anna T. Jeans Fund, the Julius Rosenwald Fund, and the John F. Slater Fund.[5]

In 1931, a bulletin published by the Texas Department of Education admitted that while black public schools in Texas had improved, much work remained:

> In many counties and school districts colored schools are inadequately supported; their terms are too short for efficient work; their teachers are ill prepared for the work; classrooms are overcrowded and woefully lacking in essential equipment; and many of the schools are housed in buildings wholly unsuited to successful school work.[6]

In Anson, Texas, the "Colored School," which had almost 150 students and only two teachers, did not begin until the cotton picking was over. "I don't know how we got anything accomplished," a student remembered. School textbooks for black students were usually discarded textbooks from white schools. One teacher, who angrily complained to her superintendent when African American students received "the old, raggedy, nasty, dirty books" that the white instructors had discarded, said that if it were up to her, "I'd throw them back at them!"[7]

## EDUCATION FOR MEXICAN AMERICANS IN TEXAS

The growing numbers of Mexicans in the region often faced the same segregation and discrimination. Although school districts often classified Mexican American children as "white," in the late nineteenth century some public schools began offering them segregated education. Thus Texas, in addition to segregating African American children, had the financial burden of some segregated schools for Mexican American students, especially in rural South Texas.[8]

Historian Arnoldo De León has carefully detailed the racial attitudes white settlers in Texas held toward Mexican Tejanos from the opening of American settlement in the nineteenth century. "They regarded Mexicans as a colored people, discerned the Indian ancestry in them, and identified them socially with blacks," De León states. "In principal and fact," he continues, "Mexicans were regarded not as a nationality related to white, but as a race apart." Following World War II, those attitudes began to undergo a sea change, and, as Amilcar Shabazz points out, it was largely because Mexican Americans were legally considered "Caucasian" and were able to constitute a "Trojan horse within the fortress of white supremacy" that helped to "soften white resistance to desegregation." Neil Foley argues, however, that this softening took place even earlier in the twentieth century, but the hyper-Americanism following World War I caused a retrenchment in attitudes, as Carlos Blanton demonstrates through changes in Texas' English-only language policy in the 1920s. Both Mexican Americans and African Americans struggled against segregation within Texas schools. Through their efforts between 1930 and 1950, the attitude of education professionals began changing toward Mexican American and African American students.[9]

During the Progressive Era, many whites based their discrimination against African Americans and Mexican Americans upon the concept of Social Darwinism. Early anthropologists believed societies evolved in certain prescribed stages. They considered Northern European societies as the most evolved "civilizations," while aborigines and Africans were "savages," the lowest form of society. They believed, however, that with the proper guidance the societies on the lower rungs could eventually climb the ladder to "civilization." Whites in Texas saw Mexican society as only slightly more advanced than that of African Americans, and they applied the same Jim Crow techniques to keep Mexicans and Mexican Americans segregated.[10] Texas A&M sociology professor William E. Garnett warned that miscegenation between poor whites, African Americans, and Mexican Americans would lead to "a large mongrel population" that would threaten the very existence of "satisfying or efficient community organizations, schools, churches, or recreational life," especially in rural areas. Ironically, Social Darwinists argued for racial segregation but at the same time advocated for improved educational opportunities for minorities. Indeed, they saw no inherent contradiction in Jim Crow's "separate but equal" requirement in the *Plessy v. Ferguson* case. Garnett could therefore call for separation of the races while at the same time decry that African American schools and their teachers often received less than half the funds of their white counterparts. "Much the same situation prevails where there are separate schools for the Mexicans," he stated. Any discussion concerning the education of minorities in Texas should consider "the fact that their living conditions are closely related to the school work" and are just as important as "conditions prevailing in the schoolroom itself." Seen as culturally and socially inferior, and subject to the demands of the harvest season, African American and Mexican American children faced a life of illiteracy and poverty, and Social Darwinists like Garnett warned that unless better and more equal educational opportunities were provided, these conditions would work toward the economic and social decline of the state.[11]

Garnett and others were concerned because in the early twentieth century the Mexican immigrant population increased dramatically. Beginning in the late 1880s, the cattle drives that had played such a large part in Texas history following the Civil War began declining with the expansion of railroads and refrigerated cars into South Texas. As midwestern farmers used those same railroad lines to move to South Texas and take advantage of the cheap available land, many saw the benefit of Mexican agricultural laborers and cattle and stock hands. Later, Texas farmers drew Mexican immigrants with the promise of agricultural employment in the state's expanding cotton fields and the mobility provided by accessible railroad transportation connecting Corpus Christi with Brownsville. As far as Mexican workers were concerned,

Texas appealed to those looking for work because they did not have to compete with Asian immigrants seeking agricultural work in California.[12]

Yet, more than any other event, the Mexican Revolution of 1910 pushed additional Mexican nationals across the Rio Grande into Texas and other states in the southwestern United Sates. A conservative estimate holds that almost 730,000 crossed the border into the United States between 1910 and 1930, but the actual numbers were probably much higher. In 1920, across the five southwestern states (Arizona, New Mexico, Colorado, California, and Texas) the Mexican American population composed 5.3 percent of the total boarder population, and 4.3 percent of the Texas populace. By 1930, Mexican Americans in the Southwest increased to 9.6 percent and to 11.7 percent in Texas. The statistics correspond to a population increase from about 100,000 Mexican Americans at the time of the 1848 Treaty of Guadalupe-Hidalgo to nearly three million by 1930.[13]

Still, while Texas farmers and ranchers welcomed the "cheap and subservient labor" Mexicans provided, white Texans wanted to restrict the immigrants' political voice. Some Texans feared permitting the Mexicans the franchise would result in an expansion of the patron system controlled by the old South Texas ranchers, and they sought to restrict Mexican participation in Texas social and political life. These restrictions eventually affected both Mexican nationals and native Tejanos. As the number of Mexican immigrants increased, Texans asked themselves three questions: Should immigration be unrestricted? Should the current immigration laws be enforced? Or should immigration restrictions be extended to limit people coming from Mexico and other South American countries, just as restrictions had been placed on immigrants from Asia and Southern and Eastern Europe?[14]

Although the border states faced the greatest influx of migrant workers, Mexican immigrants traveled as far as Cleveland and Pittsburgh in search of work. States in the Midwest and industrial cities in the Northeast opposed restrictions on potential laborers from south of the border. In 1925, U.S. Representative John C. Box, of Jacksonville, Texas, a supporter of immigration control and the National Origins Act of 1924, predicted in an article reprinted in *Texas Outlook,* that the spread of cotton into West Texas would lower the standard of living. "The cotton plant, poverty and illiteracy thrive together," he warned. Box, influenced by the Social Darwinism of the era, considered Mexicans similar to African Americans because both were "inextricably associated" with cotton production, as Garnett had stated earlier.[15]

Along a similar vein, Edward Everett Davis, dean of North Texas Agricultural College, could distinguish between Mexican immigrants and native Tejanos. He noted that native-born Mexican Americans shared a common culture with white Texans, and he noted how the difference affected education levels. Nevertheless, he claimed, "where ever the foreign-born Mexican immigrant goes, the standards of home life and education are distinctly lowered." Whites retreated in the face of the Mexicans migration north, and this had a profound effect on public schools, according to Davis:

> It is seldom that a Mexican child is seen in the white school. The white children and white parents resent their presence. This calls for a duplication of school facilities, if the Mexicans are to have free-school privileges—separate schools for the Mexicans and the whites.[16]

As an early example of what would later be called "white flight," Davis predicted that as whites left areas dominated by the increasing number of Mexican immigrants, schools would suffer from lower enrollment and disrepair, leaving only "crumbling monuments of vanishing white communities."

White Texans were not the only group who felt threatened by the increase in immigration. Middle-class Mexican Americans feared that the growing racism against Mexican émigrés would soon threaten the social and political standing of native Tejanos. Certainly, they had some justification for their fears. In the years following the Texas Revolution and the acquisition of Mexican territory following the Mexican War, Mexican Americans had seen an erosion of wealth, property, social standing, and political power in South Texas. Now as the Mexican population increased in other areas of the state, there were some Texas educators who echoed the Social Darwinism that held fairer-skinned people as socially superior to those with darker skins. Even some who considered established and middle-class Mexican Americans "white" insisted upon segregating the "dirty 'greaser'" peon children until they could "learn to 'clean up' and become eligible to better society." These educators believed in Americanization and assimilation—that the "greasers" could learn to adapt themselves to American or "civilized" culture. Once the Mexican children were assimilated, proponents argued, they should have a "fair chance at the free elementary schools of our land." The assimilationist approach was popular and considered progressive in the late nineteenth and early twentieth century when the U.S. population experienced a significant increase in immigrants. Many Progressive reformers, including Jane Addams and John Dewey, adopted this approach, believing it important to make students adapt to the majority culture.[17]

Mexican Americans took an active role to protect their status. In the 1920s, native-born Tejanos formed *sociedades mutualistas* to fight discrimination. The Mexican Protection Group (La Agrupación Protectiva Mexicana) protested lynchings and other acts of violence and discrimination against Mexicans. Following World War I, returning Mexican American soldiers formed groups stressing their Americanism. The Order of Sons of America (Orden Hijos de America) formed in 1921 as a reaction to the growth of the Ku Klux Klan in Texas and across the nation. Later, many of these middle-class Mexican American groups coalesced into the League of United Latin American Citizens (LULAC) at the end of the 1920s to consolidate their power and continued to oppose discrimination and segregation as the Mexican and Mexican American population increased.

Adequate housing was a challenge for Mexican and Mexican American school children. Both groups often found themselves living in squalor, some in crowded, dirt-floored shacks usually contained one or two rooms, without running water, doors, or windows. One observer lamented that the shacks were "hardly fit to shelter goats." This simple shelter was blind to skin color, however, for inside housing of this sort lived the southern poor, white, black, and brown. While the rents may have seemed inexpensive, ranging from $1.50 to $4 per month, even the director of the Texas Planning Board for public housing in the late 1930s, E. A. Wood, commented that those prices should have provided better accommodations. Woods lamented that many of the poor in Texas cities "reside in hovels and shacks without adequate space for ordinary household purposes, and without the necessary appurtenances for healthful living."[18]

Some associated poverty with race. Dean Edward Davis stated in a *Texas Outlook* article that African Americans were prime examples of the Malthusian belief that lower socioeconomic groups produced larger families, stating they were "more prolific in the production of children" than in "bales of cotton and bushels of corn." Davis associated Mexican Americans with the same racial characteristics. "All that has been said about the Negro regarding his low economic productivity, poor standards of living, and large family," he concluded, "apply with equal validity to the Mexicans." Segregation, poor housing, poverty, and agricultural labor all worked against Mexican families trying to increase their standards of living. These same factors contributed significantly to limiting the educational opportunities and school achievement for Mexican and Mexican American children.[19]

Mexican American children in the first half of the twentieth century often first encountered segregation in Texas public schools. Separate public schools for Mexican children were established at the turn of the century, and the practice spread as immigration spread. In 1930, the U.S. Supreme Court allowed that a lack of English proficiency could be addressed with separate classes for non-English-speaking students. The language barrier provided an excellent rationale for segregating these children into "Mexican schools." The prevailing white attitude favored grouping all Hispanics, the native-born and immigrants, together. One former student attended a mixed school in one town then a segregated school when her family moved to a larger town. She recalled, "Then, because you were a Mexican, you did not go to the white school until you were in the fifth grade because they figured you didn't know how to talk English and you couldn't get along with the [white] kids."[20] Another Mexican American stated that as a schoolboy, segregation applied to students of all races:

> They had one school for coloreds; they had one school for us, and one school for [whites]. Now, if you graduated from ours [the Mexican American school] you could not go to high school; they wouldn't let you go to high school. But then I didn't know why, and I didn't ask why, because there was nobody going to answer me anyway.[21]

Although whites rationalized that segregating the students would give the Mexican children an opportunity to learn English, this goal usually went unmet. A report published in 1933 stated that many teachers and administrators believed that "the fourth or fifth is the grade at which separate instruction for Mexican pupils should end." They based this principle upon the hope that Mexican students would learn to speak "and understand English with considerable ease" by the fourth or fifth grade. In practice, however, this was often not the case.[22]

For the most part, public school educators ignored Mexican American students. Attendance policies were lax. "Teachers didn't care if the students learned or not, or if they attended," one man remembered. "Parents didn't encourage school because they didn't know any better, or if work came into conflict with school, work won out." Mexican American schools usually received little better attention than their black counterparts did. Indeed, the 1925 Texas School Survey reported that most superintendents found the compulsory attendance law at that time unsatisfactory and did not try to enforce it. The report continued, "This was especially true in the communities in which there was a large Mexican element."[23]

Even when Mexican American children did attend school, teachers were not concerned whether Spanish-speaking children failed or passed and paid them scant attention. One observer noted that in classes composed of both Spanish- and English-speaking children, the teachers would spend most of their time working with the English-speaking children. They knew that if the white children failed, the parents would be outraged. Some parents might even blame the teacher for spending too much time with the Spanish-speaking children. On the other hand, teachers did not have to worry about repercussions from Mexican parents when their children did not advance.[24]

When Lyndon Baines Johnson, a former Texas public school teacher, became president of the United States in 1963, he made public some of the problems Mexican American students had faced in segregated schools when he was a teacher in the 1930s. Johnson served as a student-teacher and principal at the "Mexican ward"—Welhausen Elementary School—in Cotulla, Texas, for one year while he was a student at Southwest Texas Teachers College in San Marcos. This experience became one of the best-known influences for Johnson's War on Poverty and his efforts against discrimination and segregation. One of Johnson's cabinet officers said the president told this story:

> There was in Cotulla, Texas, a road stand where truck drivers stopped for breakfast. Behind it was a garbage heap. The Mexican children would go through the pile, shaking the coffee grounds from the grapefruit rinds and sucking the rinds for the juice that was left.[25]

Johnson often referred to his brief experience in Cotulla throughout his presidency. The students, he stated, "knew even in their youth the pain of prejudice."[26]

Some educators who were influenced by Social Darwinism wondered if Mexican students were capable of learning as well as white students were. Between 1915 and 1950, Mexican American students scored lower in intellectual and educational testing than whites. A 1925 master's thesis by a student at the University of Chicago concluded that it benefited Mexican students to be segregated. Based on a study of San Antonio, Texas, students, the study argued Mexican students tended to be physically older but mentally younger than other students at their grade level. They scored lower on IQ tests, failed to improve in language skills, came from a lower socioeconomic background, and did better work overall in a completely Mexican school than in an integrated or "mixed" school.

Social science theories also added to the fears that the increasing Mexican population threatened the democratic fabric of Texas. In 1925, sociologist

William Garnett stated that only when there was "homogeneity of the population, in race, wealth, education, social tradition, and religion" would the nation realize "social justice and equality of opportunity for all." He blamed "swarms of little fellows commonly seen around Mexican shacks" on encouragement of large families by the Catholic Church, and he echoed the theories of Thomas Malthus that it was a "fact that the lower the standard of living the higher the birth rate always tends to be."[27]

Reflecting the ideology of Social Darwinism compounded by the growing immigrant population in Texas, William O. Sisk in 1930 concluded that because of "language, cultural levels, and the prevailing attitudes of other people toward the Mexicans" the "Mexican child does cause a problem in the school system." With reports from educational professionals advocating segregated classes for Mexican American students, local school boards could conclude that Mexican American children were inferior to whites culturally, socially, and educationally.[28]

## EARLY LEGAL CHALLENGES TO JIM CROW EDUCATION

In Del Rio, a Texas border town one hundred fifty miles west of San Antonio, the school district passed a bond in 1930 to expand its school facilities. Mexican American parents worried that the expansion of the "Mexican" school would perpetuate segregation. Although the Texas Constitution of 1876 called for separate schools for blacks and whites, the parents argued in a law suit, since Mexican Americans were considered white, their children should not be segregated. Just three years earlier, Chinese Mississippian Martha Lum's father sued the Rosedale, Mississippi, consolidated high school district because his daughter could not attend classes with white students. The U.S. Supreme Court decided that the states could separate schools for whites and "coloreds," and that since Chinese students were "yellow," they were "colored."[29]

In the Del Rio decision, the state district court agreed with the Mexican American parents that their children should be integrated. Upon appeal, however, the San Antonio appeals court decided that schools could constitutionally segregate because of language differences. The *Del Rio ISD v. Salvaterria* decision, although a defeat, directed public attention to LULAC's struggle against Jim Crow segregation on behalf of Mexican Americans and helped promote the organization's nationwide expansion. The Del Rio lawsuit also became the first case to ask for judicial review over the way Texas schools educated Mexican American students. Even though the state classified those students as "white," it was given legal authority to segregate Mexican American students based upon language differences, but the *Plessy* decision allowed the state to segregate black students with impunity.[30]

The same year the Supreme Court issued the Del Rio decision, Nathan Margold issued a strategy report for the NAACP on confronting African American segregation in southern schools. A protégé of Felix Frankfurter, Margold had represented El Paso physician Lawrence Allen Nixon in the second case Dr. Nixon brought before the Supreme Court (*Nixon v. Condon*) challenging the "Lily White" primary. The attorney believed that despite the "separate but equal" doctrine, separate education was inherently unequal, especially in the way funds were distributed. As a result, schools for minority students were understaffed, overcrowded, and faculty members were underpaid. Instead of challenging the constitutionality of segregated schools, Margold suggested the NAACP legal team challenge southern school districts and systems to force them to provide students in segregated schools an education that was truly equal. In southern states, where educational funding was already limited, this strategy would force school districts to maintain two or, in Texas' case, three distinct school systems. Thus, NAACP attorney Thurgood Marshall employed Margold's suggestions and thereby sought to make segregation too costly for southern school districts to maintain.[31]

## THE STRUGGLE FOR EQUALIZING TEACHERS' SALARIES

Teacher salaries provided a glaring example of the inequalities in the South's Jim Crow educational system. Although it was common throughout the South for school districts to pay African American teachers less than their white counterparts in the years following Reconstruction, the salary gap increased during the twentieth century. White teachers' salaries increased after the turn of the century, yet black teachers' salaries remained the same; in some cases African American teachers' salaries decreased. White school officials justified paying African American teachers less with the tangled, circular logic born from racial discrimination. Black teachers also received less pay because they were sometimes less qualified, and most taught in rural one-room schools where the pay was generally lower. The situation was compounded because African Americans generally had fewer opportunities for higher education in southern states, in regional normal schools, and in teacher training institutions. In Texas, Prairie View was the only public teachers college for African Americans. Ironically, one teacher observed that in East Texas more black teachers held master's degrees than white teachers did.[32]

In the late 1930s, NAACP organizer Harry T. Moore led the first of many challenges to unequal pay for African American teachers in Brevard County, Florida. Throughout the decade, however, white teachers earned an average of 80 percent more than their black counterparts. In 1940, Marshall brought the case of *Alston v. School Board of the City of Norfolk* to the Fourth Circuit Court of Appeals. In the original case, the federal district court for Virginia ruled that African American teacher Melvin O. Alston knowingly and willingly accepted his teaching contract at a lower pay scale than white teachers and therefore had no remedy. The circuit court, however, overturned this decision in finding that unequal pay for black and white teachers with similar assignments violated the Fourteenth Amendment. When the Supreme Court denied the Norfolk School Board's request for a writ of certiorari, school boards around the South began working to equalize pay, some more rapidly than others.[33]

In the early 1940s, the Colored Teachers State Association of Texas, under the direction of President Leslie J. White, formed the Commission on Democracy in Education with the mission of pursuing equal teachers' salaries throughout Texas via court action. On February 24, 1943, the Commission on Democracy in Education participated in a successful case against the Dallas Independent School District, brought by Thelma Paige and the Dallas Colored Teachers Alliance, in favor of salaries equal to those of white teachers. The Commission also applied pressure to school boards in Houston, Galveston, and other Texas school districts.

In Houston, African Americans starting out in a teaching career could expect only 60 percent of their white counterparts' salary. After Paige's success in Dallas, Houston African American teachers began calling for salary equalization. In April, after they presented a petition to the school board, Houston's black teachers learned that their earnings would increase over the next two years until they matched white teachers' pay.[34]

Besides the increasing pressure on Texas educational leaders to equalize salaries for black teachers, African Americans and Mexican Americans looked for other opportunities to challenge discrimination on the eve of World War II. In mid-December 1940, Dallas resident Irving G. Lang wrote a letter to the editor of the *Dallas Morning News* condemning segregation. From 1619, when the first Africans arrived in Jamestown, through the American Revolution and Civil War, he wrote, African Americans were loyal to the nation. Yet, he complained, even as the war clouds gathered in Europe, African Americans "are not allowed to enlist in the air force, marines and Navy as a fighting unit." Lang's letter reflected a common experience for blacks across the South in the early 1940s. Although the United States began mobilizing for war before Pearl Harbor, African Americans, who had suffered disproportionately to their numbers during the Depression, faced discrimination when they answered the call for workers in war industries. Factories hired blacks to serve only in menial service jobs, usually on a "last hired, first fired" capacity.[35]

Where the United States military did allow for blacks to enlist, it kept African Americans in service positions. The navy would only allow blacks to serve in the mess halls. Texan Doris "Dorie" Miller was assigned as a mess attendant on the battleship USS *West Virginia* when the ship came under attack at Pearl Harbor. For his brave actions, Miller earned the Navy Cross in late May 1942. The next year a Japanese submarine sunk his ship, and he was posthumously awarded several medals, including the Purple Heart and the World War II Victory Medal. Despite his honors, Doris Miller died a navy cook because his skin was black. The other branches of the military also limited African American participation. Discrimination against black Americans limited more than their opportunity to fight in the war. Many wondered how anyone could claim citizenship when they could not contribute to their nation's defense?[36]

To bring their case to the attention of Pres. Franklin D. Roosevelt's administration, A. Philip Randolph, president of the Brotherhood of Sleeping Car Porters, called for a mass demonstration by African Americans from around the nation in a "March on Washington" with the message: "We loyal Negro-American citizens demand the right to work and fight for our country." Randolph worked with Walter White of the NAACP and the National Youth Administration's minority director Mary McLeod Bethune to pressure FDR to end the discrimination. The Roosevelt administration prevented the demonstration only by agreeing to address the issue of discrimination, but it was limited. Executive Order 8802 created the Fair Employment Practices Committee and forbade bigotry in defense industries under federal contract stating that "there shall be no discrimination in the employment of workers in defense industries or government because of race, creed, color, or national origin."[37]

Mexican immigrants and native-born Mexican Americans also faced workforce prejudice, but they provided a much needed labor force for Texas agriculture. In August 1942, the United States and Mexico signed the

Mexican Farm Labor Program Agreement, or Bracero Program, that allowed Mexican laborers to work, temporarily, in the United States and relieve the labor shortage resulting from the manpower demands of World War II. The labor agreement provided that both governments monitor the working and living conditions of the workers to ensure fair and humane treatment.[38]

Discrimination persisted in Texas, however, and by 1943 the Mexican government excluded Texas from participation in the Bracero Program. President Roosevelt established the Office of Inter-American Affairs (OIAA) to improve relations with South American countries during the war. The OIAA encouraged Texas governor Coke Stevenson to appoint a "Good Neighbor Commission" within the state to address the discrimination charges. The Good Neighbor Commission began work in 1945, and by 1947 Mexico lifted the ban. But, when the state commission's executive secretary, Pauline Kibbe, published a book documenting the continued adversities Mexican laborers faced in the Lone Star state, pressure from South Texas farmers influenced her decision to resign. The new director, Tom Southerland, continued to work to improve conditions for Mexican workers.[39]

## THE BATTLE AGAINST JIM CROW EDUCATION INCREASES

By 1947, public schools reflected the attention given to improving relations with Mexicans and Mexican Americans. In the California educational segregation case *Mendez v. Westminster,* a federal court determined that forcing Mexican American children to attend a segregated school violated the Fourteenth Amendment because the California educational system had no authority to separate the students. The next year, a Texas case brought by Minerva Delgado against the Bastrop Independent School District hoped to apply the same interpretation as the California case. Federal District judge Ben H. Rice determined that segregation of Mexican American students violated the Fourteenth Amendment. He did allow that students not proficient in English could be separated in different classrooms but within the same school other children attended, and only during the first grade.[40]

Perhaps the death of archsegregationist Theodore G. Bilbo of Mississippi in 1947 marked a turning point in racial attitudes across the South. That year, he had published a book in which he proclaimed:

> No government agency or organization or individual will ever convince the
> people of the South that separate schools for whites and Negroes should not

be maintained. The people of the South know that the doctrines of those who argue for the mixing of the races in the institutions of learning would lead to the destruction of all racial barriers and to the amalgamation of the races.[41]

To underscore his determination to preserve segregation, Bilbo stated that anyone who disagreed with him could "Go straight to Hell." At the same time, however, John W. Studebaker, commissioner of the U.S. Office of Education, encouraged colleges and universities to allow black students to attend classes. In 1946, Pres. Harry S. Truman appointed a Committee on Civil Rights to study the problem of discrimination. *To Secure These Rights: The Report of the President's Committee on Civil Rights* urged the federal government to take the lead in the American civil rights movement. The report suggested equal opportunity in education, employment, and housing as well as a federal antilynching law and an end to poll taxes. Civil rights violations were not just a local or state problem but reached beyond the nation to the world community:

> A lynching in a rural American community is not a challenge to that community's conscience alone. The repercussions of such a crime are heard not only in the locality, or indeed only in our own nation. They echo from one end of the globe to the other, and the world looks to the American national government for both an explanation of how such a shocking event can occur in a civilized country and remedial action to prevent its recurrence.[42]

In February 1948, the president asked Congress to implement the committee's recommendations, and even despite southern opposition, Truman moved forward on his own. On July 26, 1948, the president ordered an end to segregation of the military with Executive Order 9981. The measure directed that "there shall be equality of treatment and opportunity for all persons in the armed services without regard to race, color, religion or national origin."[43]

How other nations perceived the U.S. problem of bigotry became a matter of great concern, and some shame, for Americans who believed that the United States had emerged a superpower from a battle against the blatant racism of Nazi Germany. In a letter to Franklin Roosevelt, one African American man complained:

> We are still deprived of proper education, robbed of our vote and ruled by lynch law in the South. In the North we are discriminated against in business: forced to live in ghettos like Harlem, through housing restrictions and prejudice. We are "undesirable" socially. We can take no pride in our armed forces. . . . We can become no more than flunkies in the army and kitchen boys in the navy.[44]

If the federal government could take a proactive role in fighting discrimination at home, the nation could demonstrate tolerance to the world. But the federal government alone could not change attitudes. The states had to take responsibility for protecting the rights of their citizens.

In 1949, two events illustrated challenges to Texas segregation policies. First, in early January, a funeral home in Three Rivers, Texas, refused to hold a wake for the remains of Private First Class Felix Longoria. Although the funeral home agreed to supervise Longoria's burial, its management refused to permit a wake because they feared Mexican Americans would "get drunk and lay around all the time," and the white community would disapprove. Second, the U.S. Supreme Court began reviewing Heman Sweatt's case against University of Texas president Theophilus S. Painter over the decision to deny Sweatt's admission to the University of Texas Law School because of race.[45]

Both cases reveal that despite some progress in race relations for Mexican Americans and African Americans discrimination still persisted. In each instance, the federal government supported the rights of the minority group. In the Felix Longoria case, Texas' U.S. senator, Lyndon Johnson, arraigned a full military burial at Arlington National Cemetery. In Sweatt's case, the Supreme Court desegregated graduate and professional education.

Widespread support for a state antilynching law also reflected a change in racial attitudes. Gov. Beauford Jester, the editor of the *Dallas Morning News,* and the Texas Council of Church Women joined the supporters of the bill. The *Dallas Morning News* editor denounced mob violence as "a lawless act that the law-abiding can not with safety condone." Although it is certainly worth noting that many supported a state antilynching law to avoid the federal government passing a stricter law, the legislation indeed passed the Texas House of Representatives in 1949.[46]

Although Texas was alone among southern states passing antilynching legislation, other events reveal the ambiguity Texans had about changing the social structure. The same day the antilynching bill passed, a Dallas newspaper reported that the first African American was running for the Dallas City Council on the Progressive ticket. It also noted some discussion among white Democrats about whether or not they would permit black Democrats to attend the Texas Jefferson-Jackson Day dinners. If they did, would they be segregated? In the entertainment section, the Telenews theatre announced it would show D. W. Griffith's film *Birth of a Nation.*[47]

The story of Mexican American students Henry and Julian Nava is illustrative of the challenges to Jim Crow segregation during and after World War II. As a student at Roosevelt High School in Los Angeles, California,

Henry Nava's teachers encouraged him to take vocational rather than academic courses. "They're kind of hard," they told him. "We don't know if you want to study or concentrate that hard because you're doing so well in wood shop," they said. During World War II, Henry served in the Navy Medical Corps, and he realized that the most dangerous duty was often assigned to those without an education. During leave, Henry returned to his alma matter to make sure his younger brother, Julian, would go to college. Again, school counselors suggested a vocational course of study. Henry insisted that his brother take academic courses. Julian Nava followed his older brother's wishes and eventually completed his PhD in history from Harvard University. President Jimmy Carter later appointed Julian Nava ambassador to Mexico in 1979.[48]

Similar stories can be found in Texas. E. C. Lerma, whose parents had emigrated from Mexico, came of age in Kingsville's segregated school system. Orphaned at the age of eight, Lerma saw football as the key to continuing his education through high school and eventually to Texas A&I University in 1934. This was quite an accomplishment considering it was the height of the Depression and because of the discrimination he faced on and off the field from fellow athletes and students from other schools, who looked down upon him because of his ethnicity. After graduating, Lerma turned to teaching and coaching. He had a distinguished career as a high school coach, leading his teams to thirteen championships. When he retired from coaching, he turned to administration and eventually retired as superintendent of the Benavides school district. In 1991, the school district honored him by naming the football stadium in his honor. Historian Jorge Iber observes, "The community that in 1940 doubted whether a Mexican American had sufficient intelligence and leadership skills to pilot a football program, bestowed its greatest tribute on this one of humble Mexican origins."[49]

About the same year that E. C. Lerma enrolled in Texas A&I, a few blocks away a third grader named Sarita Cavazos became the first Mexican American student enrolled in Kingsville's Flato Elementary School. With the support of the school superintendent, the school board approved her parents' request to exempt her from attending Stephen F. Austin Elementary School, Kingsville's segregated Mexican American school. Perhaps due to the example set by E. C. Lerma, or because of her family's standing in the community (her father was the foreman of the Santa Gertrudis division of the King Ranch), Sarita Cavazos and her younger brothers reported less blatant discrimination. Her brother Laurie, however, stated that he was often involved in fights with an older boy who did not like Mexicans. The Cavazos family expected the children to attend college, and the Cavazos children followed their parents' admonition. Sarita became a teacher, her brother Richard became the U.S. Army's first Hispanic four-star general as well as head of the U.S. Army Forces Command. Another brother, Bobby, earned an impressive record as a tailback for the Texas Tech University football program in the 1950s and finished second in the nation in scoring in 1951. In 1953, he scored three touchdowns to help the Red Raiders defeat the Auburn Tigers in the 1954 Gator Bowl. Laurie, or Lauro Jr., became president of Texas Tech in 1980, and from 1988 to 1990 he served as U.S. secretary of education under Presidents Ronald Reagan and George H. W. Bush.[50]

Stories such as those of E. C. Lerma, and the Nava and Cavazos families are the exception rather than the rule. Yet they illustrate the changing opportunities available for minority children following the Depression. Despite the entrenched segregation and discrimination, African American and Mexican American students in Texas after World War II had the opportunity to be better educated than their parents. Between 1920 and 1950, some changes in the treatment of black and Hispanic students in the classroom foreshadowed the overthrow of segregation in 1954. The text of the *Brown* decision reflected the issues confronting minority education in the mid-twentieth century. The importance of compulsory attendance and increasing budgets for public education "demonstrate our recognition of the importance of education to our democratic society," Chief Justice Earl Warren wrote. Education "is required in the performance of our most basic public responsibilities, even service in the armed forces," he continued. He acknowledged the previous court cases that opened the doors of graduate education when he wrote that education prepared children for "later professional training." Twenty-five years of legal challenges to segregation in the public schools framed the 1954 *Brown* decision. Warren's opinion that states should consider education a "right which must be made available to all on equal terms" reflected an idea that had evolved during the first half of the twentieth century.[51]

President-elect George H. W. Bush held an inaugural event for public school teachers hosted by Secretary of Education Lauro F. Cavazos on January 18, 1989. Cavazos, who had attended public school in Kingsville, served as president of Texas Tech University before Ronald Reagan appointed him the first Hispanic cabinet member. Photograph G23607-12, George Bush Presidential Library, College Station.

## Chapter 4

# World War II and Texas Rural Schools

The Depression and World War II had a tremendous effect on U.S. society. The massive government effort to build a successful war machine to supply the Allies and the United States' own defense effort effectively ended the Depression. The military buildup included more than military contracts and a recruitment campaign—the United States also needed to create a military infrastructure to support and train enlistees. Across the South military training bases transformed rural areas, rural people left for urban areas in search of work in industries, and millions of young men and women donned uniforms and served in the military. Texas had had army installations and training bases since World War I, but the military expansion in the 1940s included naval yards and bases and prisoner of war camps across the state. As the war effort revolutionized Texas' economy and society, inequalities in the state's public schools became apparent and threatened to limit their efforts to provide students an education.

While the war ravaged much of Europe, the United States ended the war as the most prosperous nation in the world. Only 12 percent of Americans served in the armed forces, and aside from the attack on Pearl Harbor, the United States had suffered physically very little during the war, but she had suffered economically. First, during the Depression, people suffered from want and lack of money and jobs, then during the war Americans rationed commodities and fuels, recycled metals, and saved money by buying war bonds. The Depression taught Americans thrift and sacrifice; World War II mobilized the nation, transformed the economy, and resulted in sea change for the South and for Texas. As one writer predicted in *Texas Outlook* in early 1942, the war would "result in an opportunity to build decent standards of living for millions who have never had the right kinds of food, adequate clothing and comfortable shelter."[1]

## POSTWAR INFLUENCES UPON EDUCATION

The postwar baby boom also had an effect upon Texas. In 1947, 198,662 new-born Texans marked a significant increase from the 127,072 births in 1940, a 41.4 percent increase, according to the National Office of Vital Statistics. The same report noted that across the United States newborns totaled a record 3.9 million, and the next year, 1948, had the second highest number of births in history with and estimated 3.7 million children.[2] The fantastic growth in the birthrate meant the school rolls would swell, and the need for housing would be critical. Fortunately, in 1944 Congress passed the Servicemen's Readjustment Act, or GI Bill, to help returning military personnel integrate back into the workforce and economy. Besides paying for college or trade school, the GI Bill offered low-interest housing and business loans. The government would help expanding families finance housing.

On July 1, 1947, William Levitt, a former federal housing contractor, began building inexpensive homes on Long Island, New York. Other contractors copied Levitt's assembly-line methods for rapidly building affordable homes, and "Levittowns" became synonymous with communities of single-family homes that sprung up in the postwar years across the nation outside of cities in the "suburbs." The new homes alleviated the problems presented by the baby boom, but they created a new concern: new housing developments meant an expansion of public schools.

At the same time people began to realize the need for more school construction a large source of Texas school funding was threatened. The Tidelands Controversy, the battle over the ownership of offshore petroleum reserves aroused bitter feelings between some states and the federal government. Texas, along with several other states with a Spanish legal heritage, traditionally claimed a state's ownership of submerged land extended three leagues (approximately ten miles) offshore. In 1945, however, the federal government stated that Texas could only claim a three-mile boundary. The first lawsuit challenging the states' claims was against California. Although attorneys general for the other coastal states filed an amicus curiae brief, Texas Attorney General Price Daniel went so far as to argue before the Supreme Court on behalf of the state's claim to the three-league boundary. Ownership of the tidelands was an especially important question to the state of Texas and its public schools because the legislature had earmarked the revenues from offshore leases for the state's public school general fund. Daniel warned, "A federal victory . . . would mean the loss of millions of dollars which otherwise would go to the public school fund."[3]

The federal threat to state school funds, like the population spike, influenced state and local politics. The cleavage between liberals and conservatives in the Texas Democratic Party intensified during the gubernatorial election immediately following the war.[4] In 1946, former University of Texas president Homer Price Rainey ran for governor of Texas. He was appointed president in 1939, but he lost his position in 1944 fighting against conservative leadership on the University of Texas Board of Regents. His gubernatorial challenge was unsuccessful, however, as three conservative opponents painted Rainey as a radical who supported integration, academic libertarianism, taxation of natural resources, and unionism. Instead, voters elected Beauford H. Jester, a former University of Texas regent and Texas railroad commissioner. It was a time of many changes for the state.

The state's demographics were changing. The people of Texas, like those in the rest of the United States, once lived in predominantly rural areas, but the Depression and World War II drove, or attracted, people from rural areas into urban areas. Often, people went to look for work in cities as the call for skilled labor in the war industries attracted many from the farms. Others left because agriculture became less dependent upon stoop labor, and as a result many left the farms during the Depression: they either could no longer earn a living from the land or were driven off by foreclosure. Increasing industrialization, urbanization, technology, and better agricultural practices brought more people to the cities.[5]

Educators across the nation began preparing for the national population shift and the effect it would have on schools. The National Commission on School District Reorganization formed in 1946 as a joint effort between the National Education Association's Rural Education Department and the University of Chicago's Rural Education Project because the two groups perceived the need for a reorganization of school systems across the United States. The Reorganization Commission issued a sixteen-page preliminary report in 1947, titled *A Key to Better Education,* that previewed the results in the expanded report that was published the next year under the title *Your School District: The Report of the National Commission on School District Reorganization.*

The Commission's findings revealed how much the nation had changed as a result of the war. Between 1840 and 1940, the percentage of Americans who made their livelihood in agriculture declined from nearly 69 percent to just over 17 percent. Ironically, in the years prior to World War II, farm production increased by a third, even though over 4.5 million people left their farms in order to seek jobs in the cities during the Depression. In the first half of the 1940s, rural areas across the United States lost almost a third of their population. Rural communities saw families leave because of the Depression and the war. Many rural communities now faced extinction because for many years so many young people had left. During the Roaring Twenties across the United States, one out of every five of the young men who had grown up on farms had left for towns and cities. A greater percentage of farm girls—one out of three—had departed also.[6]

So many youth left the farms that one study of the Commission even encouraged rural schools to prepare their students for skills they would need in urban areas:

> Rural high schools should offer the education, especially in vocational fields, needed by both rural and urban dwellers, whereas urban high schools (except where rural youth expecting to enter farming attend such high schools) need not be concerned with education for farmers, farm homemakers, and rural business enterprisers. The small rural district and its small high school cannot fulfil [*sic*] this need.[7]

The American migration from farm to city was no doubt eased because of the success of Henry Ford's efforts to make the automobile more affordable. Besides contributing significantly to supporting industries such as glass, metal, rubber, and petroleum, automobiles led to a popular interest in improved roads. As Americans became more and more rooted in the culture of the automobile, the necessity for better roads increased, especially rural roads. The growing automobile sales also benefited rural mail delivery and rural school transportation. In the twenty years between the wars, automobile ownership more than doubled, from 10 percent of the population to 25 percent and from 10.5 million cars to 32.6 million. Rural road improvement projects resulted in an increase of 350 percent, from almost 400,000 miles in surfaced roads to 1.4 million. Concomitantly with the improvement in rural roads, the development of school transportation systems increased. Better transportation in rural areas meant increased attendance and larger administrative units.[8]

## EDUCATION AND DEMOCRACY

Just as the effects of World War II made dramatic changes not only in U.S. society, government, and economics, it also had a significant effect on education. Just as New Deal policies took a back seat to the war effort, many considered that in the time of national crisis educational reforms should not be placed ahead of the nation's security. Franklin Roosevelt's political adviser Harry Hopkins stated, "I see no reason for wasting time on what today are nonessentials, such as Chaucer or Latin," he wrote. "A diploma can only be framed and hung on the wall. A shell that a boy or girl helps to make can kill a lot of Japs."[9] Yet a renewed interest in public education also resulted from the war. Echoing sentiments similar to those of Jefferson and other early public education advocates, government reformers promoted education as a tool in preserving the American way of life:

> Education is the foundation for the beliefs, aspirations, and actions of the people. It is the channel through which the accumulated knowledge and cultural heritage is enriched and transmitted to future generations.[10]

In the wrong hands, however, they warned, "dictators and demagogues" could just as easily use education as a tool of enslavement and propaganda. In effect, education became a part of the U.S. war effort.[11]

The belief that education could be used to preserve American society took on added importance in the years of economic uncertainty in the 1930s and 1940s when some feared that the depression would destroy the U.S. economy. Instead, in 1940 Harvard University president James B. Conant wrote that education would preserve democracy. He informed his audience that Jefferson's concept of universal education reflected "a belief that every potential citizen in a democratic republic should receive at least a minimum of formal instruction." Throughout U.S. history, he reminded his readers, the nation had remained a "classless" society. However, the events of the first half of the twentieth century threatened to stratify society. Conant acknowledged that some people wondered, "Have we reached a point where the ideal of a peculiar American society, classless and free, must be regarded as of only historical significance?" No, he answered. Conant believed American society still possessed the ability to remain true to the Jeffersonian ideal of a free society. "A high degree of social mobility is the essence of the American ideal of a classless society," he said. Education would preserve Jefferson's ideals, he promised, not via a radical redistribution of wealth, but though "a more equitable distribution of opportunity for all the children of the land."[12]

In 1942, Conant again addressed the importance of education. By this time, the United States had entered World War II, and it became apparent to the U.S. War Department that not all youth received an equal education. Conant revealed a startling statistic: "Nearly 40 per cent of those who enter high school leave before graduation," he stated. But a high dropout rate did not cause the disparity alone. The problem, he said, was rooted in what he called "accidents of geography and of parental fortune." Just as the Depression had threatened to widen the gap between the haves and have-nots, inequality in school opportunity would result in an educated elite and ignorant masses. In order to maintain the American ideal of democracy, the United States must provide equal opportunity in education so that "a man's children might hope to show their worth." Conant concluded by stating that Americans had within their reach "a widespread system of public and private education, a miracle judged by any other country or any other age, ready for our use," which could benefit the war effort.[13]

Conant was not alone is emphasizing the necessity of maintaining our educational system during the war. Many Americans had come to believe that education was important to the survival of democracy, but the Depression and war effort taught the importance of frugality, and economic necessities demanded careful use of public funds. Public schools needed to be improved so that American youth would have a first-rate education, but waste within the system needed to be eliminated. In the years following the Depression and World War II the demand for efficiency in education became more pronounced among educational reformers. "We did all feel the depths of the responsibility that we had to try to do things for the public and to hold down the costs of government down, too," a Texas state legislator remembered.[14]

Educators recommended that the federal government play a greater role in funding and coordinating educational services in the states. In early December 1944 at the Baltimore, Maryland, meeting of the National Council of Chief State School Officers, members passed a resolution calling for each state to pass legislation "as a means of safeguarding its educational interests and welfare." The resolution suggested all programs that organized recreational activities in communities or provided lunch programs for children should be coordinated through the schools. "There is no place for separate and independent agencies at the State level," the Council stated, but "they properly belong to, and should be a part of, a comprehensive State educational program." While recognizing the longstanding principle that education was a state and local responsibility, the Council recognized that state and local funding might fall short. In that event, the national government should "participate, when necessary, in the financing of such programs."[15]

The Baltimore meeting reflected the changes World War II had on public education. Clifford J. Durr, commissioner of the Federal Communications Commission, addressed the Baltimore meeting speaking on the uses of FM radio technology in public schools. In the speech, he acknowledged many of the changes in public attitudes toward education that had evolved since the beginning of the war, and the public schools' new responsibilities. "The story of the public schools of this country," he stated, "is one of unrelenting effort to carry the benefits of education to a constantly expanding student body." The war had a tremendous effect on education, he said, noting that schools would have to "adjust and enlarge the courses of study to meet the complexities of a rapidly changing social and economic order" so they could provide "students at least a minimum of awareness of the world in which they live."[16] Part of the changing social and economic order included the consolidation of small districts and the end of the one-room school:

> In the progress away from the one-room, one-teacher schoolhouse toward the modern well-equipped school with its staff of trained teachers, its libraries, laboratories, workshops, recreation rooms, playgrounds, and bus service for children living at a distance, a tremendous amount has been accomplished in a remarkably short period of time. For this, we owe a deep debt of gratitude to the devotion, sacrifice, imagination, and hard work of our public-school teachers and officers. They have not only had the job of educating the young, but also of educating the adults in the educational needs of the young.[17]

As the first step in modifying the nation's public schools so they could accept their new roles, become more efficient, and address the changes in Americans society, members of the Reorganization Committee believed that there needed to be a uniform state public school administration model. Reformers therefore urged states to adopt a comprehensive educational system to oversee all public schools and higher education institutions within their states.

In 1944, the National Council of Chief State School Officers conducted a survey of the school organization and school boards administration of all forty-eight states. Council president Charles H. Skidmore stated in the report, "A few States are now investigating to see how they may revise their laws to approach the best State school organization." The report suggested a model where each state would be "divided into 7 voting districts giving an equitable distribution of the social, industrial and educational interests of its people." Each of these seven districts would elect or appoint a board member to a seven-year term on a rolling basis so that one member would be replaced each year. The model state board would have "general control of all the public schools and public educational institutions of the State." Although under the general coordination of the state board, individual institutions would have their own administrative boards. The report also included a prototype for a state superintendent of schools, who would be the chief executive officer of the board, although the state board would set policy and the superintendent's salary.[18]

In early December 1945, Alexander J. Stoddard, the superintendent of schools for Philadelphia, spoke at the opening session of the American Vocational Association. He stated that when the citizens come to understand "that education is a great force either for good or for evil, for war or for peace, [it] will increasingly be exploited by the nations of the world," they would begin demanding that public officials spend more on education. He worried, however, that when the war ended if Americans would abandon their concern for the education and welfare of youth. "Are we going to forget youth as soon as we no longer need them to fight in the war which we allowed to happen?" he asked. "Shall we," he wondered, "then pinch the pennies for peace where we now deal out dollars for destruction?"[19]

In the aftermath of a war seen to protect democracy from the tyranny of fascism, the United States emerged as one of two superpowers, the old empires of Europe were in tatters, and thus began a cold war between the United States and the Soviet Union. The competition between the two superpowers led to the development of a culture within the United States that emphasized the importance of the development and expansion of U.S. democracy and capitalism. School reformer John A. McCarthy began drawing attention to the role of public education in inculcating American ideals in our nation's young people:

> In a democracy, the school system is an important unit in the community. It is a far more important and efficient unit than is sometimes recognized by those who pay the bill for education, and it is a far more important unit of society than is recognized by teachers and administrators who do not recognize the importance of their function because they are too closely involved in the development of the most valuable assets of the community, the youth who are on their way to becoming the future of the Nation.[20]

## THE CALL FOR EDUCATIONAL STANDARDIZATION

Because the war effort had demonstrated several inadequacies, the potential function of public schools in preserving and acculturating Americanism within students made school reform important after World War II. Francis T. Spaulding, commissioner of education for the state of New York, wrote in the *Ladies Home Journal* that World War II "provided a crucial test of what the high schools had done and had not done for the boys and girls who had been their pupils." During the war, Spaulding headed the education branch of the War Department after having served as dean of education at Harvard University. He was among those who believed the large number of rejected military applicants during the war was proof that U.S. public schools did not adequately educate students.

Spaulding noted that studies demonstrated students were not receiving an equal education, and schools were allowing many who did not have a mastery of academic subjects "to slip by." He also complained that schools did not instill within students a sense of civic responsibility. Instead, graduates "preferred to 'let George do it,' or 'to not stick their necks out,'" he wrote. Nor were they aware of local, state, or national issues, he continued. "It was their ignorance on this latter score," Spaulding reported, "that led members of the Army and Navy command . . . to doubt that the millions of recruits had any clear idea of what they were fighting for."[21]

The lack of uniformity in public education across the nation seemed to be a major obstacle facing instructors in promoting a common culture that would instill the virtues of preserving the American way of life into school students. It was evident that children in U.S. schools did not receive an equal education, and reformers targeted the common practice of basing school funding on local property taxes. Because the value of property varied drastically from one place to another, this method of funding resulted in wide differences in school districts' income and what schools could afford to budget for education. In order to provide some balance, state governments provided supplemental revenues for schools in areas with greater needs, "equalizing funds." In wealthy areas, these state funds helped districts provide a high level of service to their students. Many poorer areas, however, still could not provide a "satisfactory" program of instruction, even with the equalizing funds. Reformers called for state education boards to develop a standardized curriculum to provide their school-aged children with what came to be termed a "minimum," "basic," or "foundation" program.[22]

Many reformers claimed that a "foundation" program would help democratize education. Dean Larry Haskew, of the College of Education at the University Texas, provided a definition of a foundation program. He explained that a minimum program meant to correct what Conant termed "accidents of geography and parental fortune." Developing a foundation program would mean that it would no longer make a difference "wherever a child is located, whoever his parents may be, and regardless of the actions in another school district," Haskew expounded, "he's going to get an opportunity that is equal to everybody else's." State leaders appreciated the promise that foundation programs held forth as Texas state senator A. M. Aikin Jr. explained, "I've always said that a kid that doesn't sit over an oil well ought to have just as much education as a kid that does sit over an oil well."[23]

In their efforts to implement a more efficient, equal, and democratic educational system reformers saw rural schools as an anachronism, a roadblock on the path to the type of school system that would address the needs of the public schools in the aftermath of World War II. As rural sociologist Lowry Nelson stated, rural institutions like the church and school "were usually too small and unspecialized for effective action." The spread of automobiles and better roads now made it easier to bring students from more isolated areas to consolidated schools. But to many who lived in rural areas, just as many had left as a result of the Depression or World War II, school consolidation meant another threat to their community's existence. The idea of consolidating smaller schools meant closing smaller schools. For some this was a violation of the idea of local control of public education. Closing the local school would be a bitter pill, a "drastic modification to conform to the new needs of modern society."[24] But, in 1941 the Southern States Work-Conference on School Administration Problems suggested that there had been a tendency to allow local communities too much control. That tendency resulted in greater waste and inefficiency. The report stated that "the state cannot guarantee an adequate minimum educational program for all children unless the program of educational need is defined comprehensively."[25]

Other rural people understood that they would have to make drastic changes in a postwar society. In 1945, Albert S. Goss, master of the National Grange, echoed the sentiment found in William Jennings Bryan's famous "Cross of Gold" speech. "The great cities," Bryan stated, "rest upon our broad and fertile prairies." He proclaimed to the 1896 Democratic National Convention in Chicago, "Burn down your cities and leave our farms, and your cities will spring up again as if by magic." But he warned, "destroy our farms and the grass will grow in the streets of every city in the country." Nearly a half century later, Gross acknowledged that a strong U.S. economy necessitated strong government, and along with it a strong farm policy. A bad farm policy would "invite a collapse so severe that the very foundations of our civilization would be threatened." A sound farm policy, he continued, would be based upon efficiency in production and marketing, but it should also include means for developing "a well educated, skilled farm population."[26]

## SCHOOL DEFICIENCIES AND THE DRAFT

The high military rejection rate was the signal event that rural public schools needed reform. As early as 1940, it became apparent that many American men were unprepared physically and mentally for military service. Although "Americans in 1940 believed that they enjoyed the best health and medical care in the world," physical examinations conducted during the military registration process belied the smugness. During the war, military boards rejected many enlistees from rural areas because of educational deficiencies. Observers blamed the high rejection rate on poor educational preparation and health services in the schools.[27]

The rejection numbers surprised everyone. Army officials expected to excuse only 2 percent of the draftees who passed the local boards. Astonishingly, even after local boards excused 40 percent for educational and physical limitations, the army dismissed yet another 15 percent. In two months during the summer of 1941 alone, over 93,000 U.S. males failed to meet the army's requirement of a fourth-grade reading level. The head of the Agricultural Adjustment Administration in Texas, B. F. Vance, responded, "it is a serious indictment of our public schools that almost 40 per cent of our boys failed to pass physical examinations for entrance into the army."[28] He noted that the state Department of Health reported before Pearl Harbor that half of the children in Texas had a poor diet, which led to other medical problems. Vance pointed out further that three-quarters of those Texans who failed the military physical examinations had problems caused by malnutrition. It seemed counterintuitive, but national reports revealed that rural areas experienced more diseases than urban areas, including "diphtheria, smallpox, mumps, scarlet fever, chicken pox and typhoid." The military reported that among potential enlistees from Texas, 20 percent had poor posture and 80 to 90 percent had decayed teeth.[29]

School reformers argued that increased attention to special needs students would help identify students with educational and health problems, while giving special attention to these students would lower truancy and discipline problems. "Education for the mentally retarded is not different in its aim from education for any group of children . . . the aim is always to make him a better and more efficient member of the group in which he lives." Texas educational reformers recommended that schools should take an active role in improving the students' health. President of the Board of Education in El Paso, Dr. E. J. Cummins, who was also a physician, stated that while many children with physical defects enrolled in schools, the schools did not do enough to improve the situation. Schools were simply not equipped to provide a basic education, he stated, because many schools had poor lighting, furnishings, heating and cooling, and lunchrooms too small to feed all the students adequately.[30]

In 1940, the Texas legislature made physical education in public schools mandatory and the state Department of Education established standards for physical education and health education classes. Yet, few school systems met the standards because the requirement was not effectively enforced. As one observer lamented about the lack of attention afforded physical education, "We have too long conceived education as consisting only of 'book learning.' We have not taken seriously the business of preparing boys and girls for that part of living which involves keeping healthy and physically fit."[31]

Apparently, though, Texas schools did not place that much emphasis on "book learning" either. The National Education Association reported that Texas had one of the highest rejection rates for military service because of illiteracy. With a national rejection rate for poor schooling at 12 percent, the Texas rejection rate was near double the national average at almost 23 percent. This placed Texas among the twelve states with high educational deficiency rates. The report noted that only South Carolina, Louisiana, Georgia, Mississippi, Alabama, Arkansas, Virginia, and North Carolina had higher rejection rates higher than Texas. Tennessee, Arizona, and Florida fared better. The NEA report connected the results to the amount of money the states spent on education—the more money a state spent on education, the fewer military rejections.[32]

The problem of illiteracy and undereducation was not limited to the South and Southwest. In 1940, the U.S. Census reported that nationally seven million citizens remained virtually illiterate; three million Americans had never been inside a schoolhouse. Five million school-age children had not enrolled in schools. Moreover, the census results confirmed that the quality of education Americans received depended upon where they were born and raised. For a typical classroom of thirty children, some school districts spent as little as $100 per year, or about $3 annually per student. A few schools could allocate as much as $6,000, or an average of $200 per student per year. John K. Norton, chair of the Department of Educational Administration at Columbia University's Teachers College, wrote that the disparity pointed out demonstrated that there was educational inequality across the nation and raised an important question, "When does inadequacy of support begin to result in inadequacy of educational opportunity?"[33]

## LOW TEACHER SALARIES AFTER THE WAR

In January 1946, *Texas Outlook* noted another problem facing the establishment of good schools—low teacher salaries. A subcommittee of the TSTA Committee on Organizational Affairs passed a resolution demanding that "the Legislature of Texas continue to make provisions for increasing teachers' salaries to the level comparable to that paid other professions." In support of the resolution, numerous articles appeared in the *Texas Outlook* illustrating the low wages Texas schoolteachers received.[34]

Following the war, teachers' salaries were the topic of conversation across the nation. An article reprinted from the *Christian Science Monitor* stated that teaching professionals across the country should receive comparable salaries to other professionals. "Teaching has always been underpaid. Teachers should be paid as well as lawyers, writers, or actresses," the writer stated. In an article reprinted from *Reader's Digest,* "Teacher's Pay—A National Disgrace," Robert Littell wrote that in Flint, Michigan, a starting teacher received $400 less than a beginning garbage collector, while in Salt Lake the city dogcatcher earned almost $7,000 more annually than a teacher with sixteen years of experience.[35]

In the 1944–1945 school year, half the nation's teachers made less than $1,800; half of those earned less than $1,200. Some 25,000 educators made less than $600 per year. Littell reported that low teachers' pay led to a high turnover rate, making teaching "not a profession, but a procession." As reported in *South Carolina Education,* one mother warned her daughter against becoming a teacher. "You take the teachers here in town. The only difference between them and Christian martyrs is the date, and lack of bonfire. I'd just as soon be a plowmule," she wrote.[36]

Another article warned professionals not to allow the state to take control over their occupations or it would become a "socialized profession" like teaching. Because of this socialization teachers received small salaries; only ministers were paid less. The low pay also led to a gender reversal in the teaching profession, the article complained. Men had been driven out of the field because teaching "is the best paid profession for women; the lowest for men." Increased red tape had also driven good educators out of the profession.[37]

While other professionals retained control of their trades, teachers could be "bossed by the general public," an article continued, and teachers were subject to the whims of politics. An elected school board "hires and fires" teachers, and under this arbitrary system "many a school board every few years enjoys an orgy of cleannig [*sic*] out the teaching staff from top to bottom," yet the administrators who supervised teachers were out of touch with classroom theories and practices. "I think, this may have been a major reason for the popularity of such fads as progressive education," he grumbled, "the old boys had been away from the classrooms and direct contact with actual children for so long they no longer knew what kids were like."[38]

More importantly, journal articles pointed out that low teacher pay had serious repercussions beyond the teachers' pocketbooks, but it also directly influenced the students as well. Low pay threatened to cause a shortage of teachers after the World War II because educators returning from active service could find other occupations that paid more. B. B. Cobb wrote: "Teachers discharged from war service are, therefore, going into business, into industry, or into some branch of government service." The flight of teachers from public education resulted in less qualified personnel in the classrooms. "Thousands of boys and girls are being deprived of their right to have the best instruction at the hands of the best prepared and the best endowed teachers," said Cobb in a 1946 article in *Texas Outlook*.[39]

If local schools and districts did not allocate more money to attract better-qualified instructors, schools would continue to struggle to find good teachers or would be forced to resort to hiring uncertified teachers. For example, during the war, Houston schools faced serious problems when the loss of almost 200 teachers by 1943 left many instructors in the classroom who were unprepared or untrained for the classes they taught. If the urban schools in Texas had problems staffing teachers, the situation was compounded for rural schools, which often had little choice when looking to solve the teacher shortage that followed the war. Teachers found that by choosing to leave the school bell and inkwell behind they stood to gain more pay, better job security, and less public scrutiny.[40]

## EQUALIZING SCHOOL FUNDS

States did allocate more money to education following the Depression and World War II. The amount of expenses per pupil in daily attendance increased across the nation from the late 1930s into the 1940s. In Alabama, the amount went from $34 in 1937–38 to $99 ten years later. Arizona, Connecticut, and Ohio doubled their expenditures in the same time span. Texas went from $71 to $197 per school-age child in attendance from the 1938 school year to the 1948 year, an increase from thirty-fourth to eighteenth in the nation. Yet the increase was misleading. Some of the increase resulted from inflation. Although the amount of the states' budget to education increased, the increase proved deceiving. Compared to Texans' personal income, the amount dedicated to educating Texas children dropped from 3.3 percent in 1937–38 to 2.8 percent in 1947–48.[41]

Despite the increase in school allocations, distribution of funds also continued to be a problem. For example, the method used by State Superintendent L. A. Woods to distribute Equalization Funds to the smaller districts through deputy superintendents across the state had raised some complaints. In the eyes of some administrators, the deputy superintendents constituted a virtual political machine that worked to support Woods's reelection campaigns. Critics said the deputies' support of Woods was self-serving since his reelections ensured the stability of their positions. Additionally, the state legislature had on more than one occasion investigated allegations of improprieties in the state textbook selection process, including payoffs from textbook companies to members of the state Textbook Board.[42]

Critics also disapproved of the existing system of state funding. In 1948, the Equalization Aid Law allowed $300 per teacher annually that could be applied for all school upkeep, administration, and day-to-day running of schools, but still many districts ran deficits from keeping schools well-equipped and maintained. For example, in 1948 the transportation budget fell short in Clay County, southeast of Wichita Falls, even with increased state transportation funding. The district superintendent hoped for additional state aid, but the Equalization Aid Law did not provide the needed relief. The appropriations came nowhere near providing the amount of money school districts needed, thus leading to the deficit. Superintendent J. B. Bright of Johnson County summed up in a letter just how important the equalization funds were to local school districts: "It is imperative that we have a liberal equalization bill if the rural and small independent schools are to be able to operate efficiently."[43]

Bigger allocations and budgets did not necessarily translate into more money for schools, Frank W. Richardson explained in 1948. He acknowledged that even though "the legislature did make substantial, although inadequate, increases in teachers' salaries, the general public believes that all our schools have plenty of money for all their school needs." An idea he found plainly wrongheaded. "Possibly some few schools do have [enough]," Richardson allowed. "However, most of them do not, and Equalization Aid Schools in particular are facing a serious financial problem."[44]

## UNEQUAL DISTRIBUTION OF FUNDS

Another problem arose concerning the method of distributing the Equalization funds. The state apportioned funds according to the number of school-age children in the school district, not based on how many children actually attended school. Reformers in other states suggested that funding should be based upon a school's "average daily attendance." Allocating funds according to attendance would cause opposition in some areas, one man pointed out, because "there is a strong tendency for school districts where attendance is low to depend on state funds almost entirely for the support of their schools and to enjoy very low rates of taxation." A change would anger landowners in these districts because they "would not be very enthusiastic about improving conditions of enrollment if it meant increases in local taxes."[45] Even worse, and giving rise to charges of graft and corruption, some observers noted there were districts that operated no schools but still received funding. Texas state senator James E. Taylor stated that he believed

> the black kids ought to be taught even if they were taught down in the park where their school was in my hometown. They ought to be taught and [school officials should not misuse] the money collected for teaching [black children] to hire teachers for the white schools which is what happened in my school district.[46]

Likewise, he felt that some districts claimed funds for Mexican American students but did not provide the schools. After checking the school rolls in the Rio Grande Valley schools, Taylor discovered one Mexican American family that appeared in the census rolls of seven counties because as they migrated throughout the state: "somebody got their name and they were listed. . . . They were migrant workers that came from the Valley and went up through Amarillo going to Idaho to pick potatoes." Critics of the Equalization Fund complained it "contributes little toward education." Others hoped that with minor adjustments to the criteria for apportionment, however, equalization could become a reality.[47]

While the problems with the system of state educational administration may have led many to lack faith in the school system, increased teachers salaries remained the primary interest of the Texas State Teachers Association. More important, state lawmakers also realized that Texas public school teachers remained underpaid and underappreciated. When he was a still a state representative from Lubbock, former Governor Preston Smith used to respond when asked, "How do you stand on the teacher pay raise?" Smith replied with two questions: (1) "How many of you here have ever known a school teacher to get rich on what the state paid him?" and (2) "Who else in your community had more influence in raising your child than a school teacher?"[48]

The times favored Texas school reformers as other states across the South were also in the process of reorganizing their state school systems. The 1948 National Governors' Conference proposed a study of the states' educational systems. Under the direction of Francis S. Chase of the University of Chicago, the report proposed six improvements needed in the state systems: (1) an investigative body, (2) a state policy-making agency, (3) local school districts large enough to be cost-effective while maintaining local control, (4) the assurance of trained, professional state and local administration, (5) hiring and retaining qualified teachers, and (6) an equal and sufficient distribution of state funds with measures for sound management and local control. This final provision seemed especially necessary since some states "may still distribute money on an unsound basis such as the school census," as Texas did. The report described this method of finance as "obsolete and inequitable."[49]

World War II had clearly influenced national and regional trends in education. The war demonstrated the need for increased standardization in public education and renewed the emphasis on the role of education in preserving democracy. During the war, gaps between rural and urban education became increasingly obvious, and rural schools across the nation faced problems of consolidation. As the rural people of Texas came to recognize this fact, their state representatives increasingly saw rural schools as inadequate. Once considered a rural state, by 1950 Texas had become an urban state. Rural communities began to lose hegemony in Texas as the agricultural regions lost citizens during the economic hardship of the Depression and the wartime mobilization of World War II.

At the time of the governors' report, Texas lawmakers, citizens, business leaders, and educators busily attempted to address some of the problems and criticisms public schools faced after World War II. Would the Texas educational reformers find a way to incorporate the study's recommendations into the legislation under consideration? One legislature noted that Texas "was a latecomer among the states that had taken over the view that education is a state responsibility rather than a local responsibility."[50] Nonetheless, Governor Jester commissioned a study to investigate solutions to the teacher-funding problem. The effort resulted in a sweeping reform of the state's educational system.

In 1943, Roy Stryker, who directed the government photography program for the Farm Security Administration and later the Office of War Information, assigned photographer John Vachon to document rural life in San Augustine. Vachon included several photos of children and provide some indication of how classroom were organized. Note how students are posed around posters of the war effort. Library of Congress, Prints & Photographs Division, FSA-OWI Collection, LC USW36-830; LC USW36-831; LC USW36-832; LC USW36-833; 834.

*Chapter 5*

# THE GILMER-AIKIN LAWS

Former Speaker of the Texas House of Representatives Claud Gilmer remembered the limitations of his high school education. He came from a family of Methodist ministers, "I had an uncle who was a Methodist minister [and] I had a grandfather that was a presiding elder, Methodist presiding elder." His mother wanted him to follow their example: "So when I finished high school up here in Rocksprings, why, she immediately decided she wanted me to go to a Methodist school in Georgetown, Southwestern University."[1]

When he looked into applying at Southwestern, "the first thing I learned was I couldn't go. My [high] school wasn't affiliated." Administrators promised him that if he passed the entrance examinations he could sit for classes: "So I sit here all August taking the entrance examinations, and finally they handed me one I hadn't even had the subject in, some kind of science. So I just quit." This experience formed his later opinions about the state of Texas rural education: "I could realize that the small, isolated school districts, if they just kept going on like that, why, how could a kid from out here get an education?"[2]

Claud Gilmer understood from personal experience that rural children often had a difficult time completing their formal education—or they quit school. Like other legislators who recognized, some from personal experience, the limitation rural schoolchildren faced, Gilmer and other lawmakers planned to use the post–World War II wealth to fund rural public schools and provide salary increases to attract and retain qualified teachers.

## THE LEGISLATURE ADDRESSES TEACHERS' SALARIES

Improving the state's rural schools remained a priority for many Texas teachers as well, and TSTA president Elizabeth Koch argued that increased teachers'

salaries and funding benefited the rural children of Texas. "Much progress
has been made," she allowed, "but there remains much still to be done,"
including raising teachers' salaries. Higher wages would help keep qualified
teachers in rural areas because they would not have to seek better pay in urban areas. "The boys and girls at the cross-roads, on the farms, in the small
towns are entitled to good teachers," she wrote, "to enough teachers, and
to all other facilities that will give them a full, broad education worthy of a
citizen of the United States."[3] It is important to point out, however, that the
low pay was not necessarily due to poorly qualified teachers in rural areas,
as some thought. In 1947–48, well over half of Texas teachers had at least a
bachelor's degree and 13 percent had a master's degree; only 18 percent had
not completed a degree. If critics wondered whether teachers really deserved
a pay raise, Sarah Gaskill in the *Texas Outlook* encouraged educators to stand
firm in their demands:

> Teachers should make no apology for requesting improved salary schedules.
> They should not apologize for seeking to improve their economic status but
> should unblushingly insist upon fair compensation. Teachers should not forget,
> nor allow the public to forget, that no work is more important than teaching.[4]

In January 1947, as the Fiftieth Legislature convened, state representative
Dallas Blankenship introduced two bills supported by the Texas State Teachers Association to the House docket to address the teacher pay issue. First,
House Bill 300 proposed to raise schoolteachers' salaries to a minimum of
$2,000 per school year, with additional compensation based upon experience
and level of education—a bachelor's degree or higher. Next, House Bill 301
was an appropriations bill to fund his proposed salary increase. In the past,
the moneys to support educational financing, including teachers' salaries,
came from the school fund. The apportionment had increased to $46 per
child in 1946, and Blankenship's funding bill called for a per pupil apportionment of $55. His proposal would have supplemented the available school
fund by allocating money from the state's general fund.[5]

On February 25, 1947, the House passed the bills, but the proposed burden on the state's general fund aroused the interest of Senate Finance Committee Chair James E. Taylor from Navarro County. On March 4, 1947,
Senator Taylor introduced an alternate bill to counter Blankenship's funding
proposal, and Rep. Claud Gilmer introduced a companion bill in the House.
Senator Taylor's bill sought to protect the general fund by suggesting that
only needy school districts should receive additional funds above the previ-

ous $46 per child apportionment. Additionally he suggested school districts receive moneys only for the number of students actually in attendance in the public schools. Although the Taylor-Gilmer bills did not challenge the proposed increase in teacher pay—only the method by which the legislature would fund the salary increase—the teachers' association immediately began mobilizing a public relations campaign.[6]

On March 8, 1947, the Texas State Teachers Association published a bulletin accusing Taylor of conspiring with special interest groups to defeat Blankenship's proposal to increase teachers' salaries. The mimeographed dispatch urged teachers to educate themselves about the issues in order to support the TSTA's efforts to lobby the legislature to approve the Blankenship bills. Taylor maintained that he was not opposed to the salary increase, as the teacher's association claimed. Instead, he believed that the Blankenship plan would unfairly benefit city school districts because urban areas would receive more funds since they had a larger school-aged population. "Then, in order to keep up with the cities, you had to pass a rural aid bill for all the other districts" to equalize the funds, he explained. Taylor was among those who believed that the rural funds were not distributed according to need but according to the state superintendent's patronage system. According to Taylor, Woods allocated the money "substantially along the lines that [he] wanted, and that was where he got the most votes. . . . I thought that was a sorry method of financing public education."[7]

Three days after the TSTA distributed the bulletin, Gilmer proposed a resolution to create a committee to investigate possible reforms to the public school system that would develop an "adequate, improved, uniform school program for Texas" with "uniform and adequate local support."[8] On April 19, 1947, Texas governor Beauford Jester publicly supported Taylor's financing plan and Gilmer's resolution in favor of an investigative committee. He also noted that Senator A. M. Aikin, an advocate of public education, would sponsor the resolution in the Senate.[9]

In 1947, when selection for the investigative committee began, members of the House, the lieutenant governor, and the governor each appointed six members, along with three representatives and three senators. The committee was formed in July. Five members had been public school superintendents: state representative Ottis E. Lock, C. B. Downing, J. W. Edgar, H. A. Moore, and H. W. Stilwell. There were former college of education administrators: B. F. Pittenger, former dean of college of education at the University of Texas, and R. J. Turrentine, formerly chair of the department of education at Texas State College for Women, served on the committee. Representative Rae Files

Still and Nan Proctor were classroom teachers. R. L. Thomas had served on the board of regents for the Texas State Teachers Colleges, and Jesse Guy Smith had been president of the Texas Congress of Parents and Teachers. Other members included Texas state senators A. M. Aikin, James E. Taylor, Gus Strauss, and Representative Claud Gilmer. Finally, Peyton L. Townsend of Dallas's Metropolitan Building and Loan Association, J. C. Peyton of Peyton Packing Company in El Paso, and Houston lawyer Wright Morrow represented the Texas business community. The committee thus represented an assembly of professional educators, lawmakers, and classroom teachers. At the first meeting in July, Governor Jester named the committee the Gilmer-Aikin Committee.[10]

## A. M. AIKIN AND CLAUD GILMER

A. M. Aikin Jr. was born on October 9, 1905, at Aikin Grove in northwest Texas, some five miles south of Clarksville, in Red River County. He was the eldest of eight children. His father owned the A. M. Aikin General Mercantile Store in Milton, where he sold goods on credit to area cotton farmers.[11] To encourage their son's education, the Aikin family sent the younger A. M. through the ten grades in Milton schools, then on horseback to Deport for the eleventh grade.

A. M. Jr. wanted to become a doctor, but the economic downturn following World War I changed his plans. As the price of cotton spiraled downwards, the farmers who had taken credit at the Aikin Mercantile gave notice that they could not pay. Welma Aikin later said of her father-in-law, "when the cotton crops failed, then he failed because they couldn't pay him."[12] As a result of the economic crisis, A. M. Jr. took a job as a clerk in the men's department at Arthur Caddel's department store in Paris, Texas.[13] One of the other employees had a daughter named Welma. He and Welma exchanged vows in 1929.[14]

In 1932, Aikin won a seat in the Texas House of Representatives. He served as a state representative until elected to the state Senate in 1936, where he served until 1979—the longest tenure of any state legislator. In 1963, his colleagues awarded him the title "Dean of the Texas Legislature." His long service to the state gained him the respect of other members of the Senate. When the legislature was not in session, he worked in a haberdashery he co-owned with his brother, and he managed a law practice in Paris.[15]

Former state senator James Taylor remembered Aikin as a legislator who people concerned with Texas politics could turn to for advice. When the sponsor of a bill came to Aikin to seek his counsel on various issues, Aikin would relate "a personal experience with a similar incident or similar situation that didn't work out like they anticipated." He enjoyed sharing the benefit of his experience in public service, and if his advice was not solicited, he might wait until after an action was taken and then would turn to his colleague and say, "Now you just got through making the worst mistake you've ever made since I've been here." While he had a reputation for even-temperedness, Taylor remembered, Aikin might "get mad, but you have an awfully hard time finding out about it." He seldom complained, and most people remembered him as "a gentleman." One colleague recalled that Senator Aikin responded to criticism graciously: "I don't think it gets him greatly upset if someone disagrees with him."[16]

The special privileges offered people in politics did not seem important to Aikin, who was once called "the biggest cheapskate in the legislature" for spending the least on office operations. When the legislative session ended, he closed his office and did not hire a secretary between sessions. "People know where I am," he said. "People don't come down there [to Austin] to see a secretary. They come to see you." Lawmakers wanted to honor him for his service, and in 1973, on A. M. Aikin Day, a senator called Aikin's brother for advice. "They wanted to give him a Lincoln Continental," Dean Aikin remembered, but he warned the senator that his brother would not accept a new car. Senator Jack Hightower suggested they present it to Welma, but Dean objected. "Oh, no, Jack," he said. "Come up with something more original than that." In the end, senators established scholarships at Paris Junior College in Aikin's honor.[17]

Only once did a question of Aikin's ethics and morality come into question. In his first term in office, the representative with whom Aikin shared a desk noticed him entertaining a young woman. The thought of this young freshman representative capering about troubled Aikin's desk mate so much that he went back to his hotel and confided to his wife, "I have never been so disappointed in anybody in my life as I have young Aikin." He explained, "The last two or three days, there's been a gal sittin' down there at his desk day and night." When his wife assured him that the young woman was indeed Aikin's Welma, suspicions ended.[18]

Like Aikin, Claud Gilmer taught school in his rural community. Also like Aikin's, Gilmer's father was a businessman who built one of the most successful independent telephone companies in Texas. After he graduated in 1919 from high school in his hometown of Rocksprings, and the brief stint at Southwestern University, he went to Meridian Junior College in Bosque County. Like Southwestern, Meridian was a Methodist institution that trained young men for the ministry. After college, Gilmer returned to Rocksprings High School as a teacher. He taught for two years and then spent another one and a half year as the principal. While principal, he also coached the school's first football team. "Daddy brought football from college to Rocksprings High School," his daughter remembered. "He was the first athletic coach we had here." When he was twenty-three, he became county judge of Edwards County. The next year he began studying law under the tutelage of the county clerk, and he eventually opened his own law practice. In 1938, when his friend Representative Coke Stevenson ran for Texas lieutenant governor, Gilmer successfully campaigned for Stevenson's vacant seat. He served in the Texas House for five terms, and he was speaker during the Forty-ninth Legislature. He was known for his support of farm-to-market roads and conservative approach toward state spending.[19]

## THE WORK OF THE GILMER-AIKIN COMMITTEE

On August 29, 1947, the committee approved a working agenda outlining its goals: study (1) the organization of the state's educational system, (2) the organization of local school boards, (3) methods of school financing, (4) teacher certification and pedagogical issues, and (5) administrative topics. It appointed subcommittees designated to study each of the five subject areas.[20]

On September 19 and 20, the chair of the state Board of Education and State Superintendent of Public Schools Littleton A. Woods came before the committee. The Board of Education suggested that the state's system of supervision needed to be unified, that members of the state board should remain appointed, and that the position of superintendent also should be appointed. Woods argued that the office must remain an elected position. On September 29, 1947, he provided a detailed report that showed that most states elected their public school superintendents.[21]

Two advisers played instrumental roles in providing information and resources to the Committee: Lawrence Haskew, of the University of Texas, and Edgar L. Morphet. Haskew previously had worked with the development of a foundation program in Florida and suggested Morphet's name to the Committee. Morphet had taught and administered in Indiana rural schools and in the Philippines. He became director of administration and finance for the state education departments in Alabama and Florida. From 1945 to 1947, he was executive secretary of the Florida Citizens Committee on Education, and he became chief of school finance for the United States Office of Education.[22]

Hollis A. Moore was another adviser who influenced the Committee. Moore became the executive agent for the Gilmer-Aikin Committee in December 1947 after he resigned as superintendent of the Kerrville school district. Moore recently had completed his doctoral dissertation at the University of Texas under the direction of B. F. Pittinger, a Gilmer-Aikin Committee member. While in Kerrville, Moore passed along information he collected for his dissertation, "Equalization of Educational Opportunity and the Distribution of State School Funds in Texas," to local state representative Claud Gilmer. Moore "had a lot of real solid, basic . . . theories as to how you'd go about improving our public school education in Texas," Gilmer explained. Moore's advice was influential in the bills Taylor and Gilmer introduced as an alternatives to Blankenship's bill to fund the teacher salary increase. By July 1948, however, Moore resigned from the Gilmer-Aikin Committee to accept a local superintendency in Colorado, and Pat Norwood of the Southwest Texas State Teachers College became the committee's executive agent.[23]

Beginning in early 1948, on Morphet's advice, the committee began to organize five advisory groups as well as a county commission in each of Texas's 254 counties to advise the Gilmer-Aikin Committee. Any interested group could nominate local members, and local committees were encouraged to solicit suggestions from Parent Teacher Associations, fraternal and social associations, local chambers of commerce, and other groups. The Gilmer-Aikin Committee chair would approve the final membership. To facilitate the work of these various teams, the Gilmer-Aikin Committee published reports, pamphlets, suggestions, questionnaires, and press releases to publicize the work of the ad hoc committees through the spring and summer of 1948.[24]

Besides professionals and lay members, the county advisory commissions were encouraged to include local media representatives. Additionally, local committees were encouraged to nominate African American representatives. "We note that in a few counties negro citizens were nominated to membership on the local committees," Moore wrote in a letter to county advisory committees. "In each instance we approved these persons. We feel that the appointment of negro citizens on the committee can contribute to

a better understanding of the educational program where the racial problem is involved," he stated. "We believe the educational opportunities available to negro children is one phase of the public school problem all of us
must consider."[25]

In the fall of 1948, Taylor called a general meeting of the Gilmer-Aikin
Committee to consider a draft proposal based on the work thus far. The
September meeting led to the publication of a booklet titled *To Have What
We Must*. The booklet contained thirty-three proposals for the county advisory committees to discuss and then report community feedback to the
Gilmer-Aikin Committee. The proposals were grouped into six general areas: (1) two proposals establishing a minimum foundation program; (2) six
proposals funding the program; (3) six proposals allowing for the reorganization and restructuring of local schools; (4) nine proposals reorganizing
and restructuring the state public education management; (5) five proposals
relating to teacher salaries, training, and certification; and (6) five miscel-
laneous proposals relating to mandatory attendance laws, student census,
textbook selection, building safety guidelines, and a recodification of the
state's school laws.[26]

Although the local county committees received the proposals in September, they had until November to report feedback to the proposals. The short
response time for public opinion provided little opportunity for the Committee to compile the reports from the county advisory committees and the
general public before the regular session of the legislature opened in January.
The committee requested Governor Jester call a special session of the legislature to consider the proposals exclusive of other legislative issues. A special
session would also allow Representatives Lock, who besides being a former
school superintendent had served as chair of the House Education Committee, and Gilmer to play effective roles in securing support for the proposals
since neither would be in the next legislature.[27]

In November, Chairman Taylor approached both Lieutenant Governor
Allan Shivers and House Speaker William O. Reed to request a special session
to consider the proposals. Superintendent Woods opposed the idea of a special session, stating that Texans "do not want this program forced down their
throats." Governor Jester agreed with Woods and declined to call a special
session. In retrospect, Rae Still wrote, the committee had difficulty preparing bills to address the proposed reforms by the start of the regular session in
January 1949, so a special session in December would have been impossible.
"Proposing changes in the existing laws is an easy matter," Rae Still wrote.

However, "writing bills to effect those changes is an entirely different and an extremely more detailed and tedious undertaking."[28]

Through 1947 and 1948, the views of some Gilmer-Aikin Committee members aroused concern, and even opposition. Primarily, it was Senator James E. Taylor's participation on the committee that raised many eyebrows. At its first meeting in late July 1947, committee member B. F. Pittinger suggested that Taylor's chairmanship would threaten the committee's work. "He made a speech . . . that I would be the worst guy in the world to have as chairman of the committee," Senator Taylor remembered. Taylor's commitment to the reformation process quickly calmed the suspicions of the Gilmer-Aikin Committee members; however, the public still had some questions.[29]

The Texas State Teachers Association also distanced itself from the committee's meetings and proposal process. Besides Taylor's conservative reputation, other members of the committee had been closely associated with the conservative, anti–New Deal, anti-Roosevelt Texas Regulars, especially Claud Gilmer. Moreover, when Taylor informed the public that he would become the public relations director with the conservative Texas Manufacturers Association after the Fiftieth Legislature ended, his traditional economic beliefs were confirmed. Therefore, when members of the Gilmer-Aikin Committee met with teachers groups to discuss the reforms under consideration, they spent a good deal of time defending Taylor's and Gilmer's involvement on the committee.[30]

To improve relations with the state's teachers, Taylor attended the Texas State Teachers Association annual convention in Dallas just a few days after the November 1948 Gilmer-Aikin Committee meeting. At that time, committee members still hoped the governor would call a special session of the legislature to consider the recommendations before the regular session began in January. Since some members of the Gilmer-Aikin Committee also served as delegates to the Texas State Teachers Association convention, the Committee encouraged them to attend the teachers' convention and solicit the TSTA leadership to pressure the governor to convene a special session. Committee members later dropped the idea because of the lukewarm reception by the TSTA to the committee's proposals. Then, Senator Taylor informed the incoming TSTA president Joe C. Humphrey that he welcomed any assistance the TSTA officers and legislative committee would provide drafting the final reform proposals. The thirty-three proposals were crafted into three revised bills, which became known as the Gilmer-Aikin Bills, officially Senate Bills 115, 116, and 117.[31]

## THE GILMER-AIKIN LEGISLATION

Senate Bill 115 established and defined the Central Education Agency composed of the state Board of Education and the state Board for Vocational Education, the commissioner of education, and the state Department of Education. The twenty-one elected members of the state Board of Education would represent each of the state's congressional districts. Senate Bill 116, the Foundation School Program Act, created the Minimum Foundation School Program, a plan to equalize education by guaranteeing each school-age child in the state a minimum, standardized education and a nine-month academic year. The final bill, Senate Bill 117, transferred funds from the Omnibus Tax Bill to pay for the foundation program. The money would go into the Minimum Foundation Fund directed by the Foundation School Fund Budget Committee. This oversight committee consisted of the state commissioner of education, the state auditor, and the comptroller of public accounts.

On January 25, 1949, sponsors introduced the three Gilmer-Aikin bills in the Senate and had them referred to the Senate Education Committee. Four senators on the Gilmer-Aikin Committee also served on the Texas Senate Education Committee, placed there by Lt. Gov. Allan Shivers, a friend of Sen. James Taylor. As president of the Senate, Shivers deserved much credit for the quick action on the Senate version of the Gilmer-Aikin Bills. The Gilmer-Aikin Committee filed its final report for printing in the *Senate Journal*. A few days later, on February 8, the Senate Education Committee held a public hearing to allow proponents and opponents to voice their opinions on the bills before a fully crowded Senate chamber. The next day the committee reported favorably on the bills. Because Governor Jester proclaimed the Gilmer-Aikin Bills an emergency measure, they came quickly before the Senate on February 15.[32]

When the Senate met to consider SB 115, Sen. Robert Kelley filibustered from three o'clock in the afternoon until eleven o'clock that evening. He raised an objection to the appointed superintendent, a proposal that many found offensive. Despite the filibuster and an attempt to attach an amendment to the bill, however, the bill passed unchanged on February 17. Consideration on SB 116 began on February 22. On Wednesday, February 23, SB 116 passed after senators approved three amendments written to protect the number of teachers, provide transportation funds, and remove the limit on transporting only public school students or personnel on public school transportation for rural areas, especially in West Texas. The final bill, SB 117, passed the Senate with little discussion and without amendments on Tuesday, March 8.

William Moore, the freshman senator from Bryan in 1949, remembered, "there was considerable opposition in the Senate" to the Gilmer-Aikin proposals. The cost of the program alone aroused some opposition in the Senate to the bills. The opposition, however, did not present a serious threat to the passage of the bills. "I don't think there was ever any doubt about its passage," Senator Moore remembered. "I think there was some that protested it, and I don't recall how many. There weren't many, but it was not a unanimous vote."[33] Despite the opposition to the bills, many realized that the existing system would not work and needed to be changed. Senator Taylor explained:

> I didn't like a politician running the school system. I thought it ought to be a professional educator. I didn't like the governor appointing the State Board of Education. I thought they ought to be elected by the people from the districts like they are now, like the Gilmer-Aikin legislation set it up. I didn't like the way the textbooks were handled. There was a lot of funny business connected with textbook adoption.[34]

## OPPOSITION TO THE GILMER-AIKIN BILLS IN THE HOUSE

Overall, supporters were surprised at the limited opposition raised against Gilmer-Aikin in the Texas Senate. The president of the League of Women Voters of Texas sent a note to Senator Taylor hoping that "sledding" the bills through the House would be as smooth. The reforms, however, faced much greater opposition and organized resistance to the bills, which threatened their passage for three and a half months, from mid-February to early June 1949.[35]

Many opponents feared that the consolidation of rural schools that Gilmer-Aikin encouraged signaled the end of rural schools—and would be the harbinger of death for rural communities. "If the rural school is abolished," warned a citizen, "along with it may go the rural church, and most of the rural activities. IS THIS THE BEST FOR THE FUTURE OF OUR COUNTRY?" The state Department of Education opposed the consolidation proposal. Senator Aikin and other Committee members did not believe a plan of consolidation needed to be included in the proposed bills. A rural schoolteacher wrote Governor Jester, "The school is the life of any community. We have watched neighboring communities die because their schools were disbanded." Instead, the teacher recommended increased governmental aid for rural schools, making them more attractive to teachers by offering better salaries, and better-equipped facilities and classrooms would attract both teachers and students.[36]

Littleton A. Woods, superintendent of public instruction from 1932 until 1950, opposed the Gilmer-Aikin legislation as unnecessarily seeking too many changes, just as he had opposed O'Daniel's proposals a decade earlier. Indeed, of all the opponents of Gilmer-Aikin, none posed so serious a threat as did L. A. Woods. Born in 1884 near Burkesville, in Newton County, Woods grew up in a farm family. He worked his father's farm until he turned sixteen, and he then began farming for himself. Like A. M. Aikin, Woods also considered becoming a doctor, but after the passage of a law that required four years in medical school, he became discouraged and turned instead to teaching. He began teaching in rural schools in 1905, the year Aikin was born. Woods worked his way through Baylor University as a farmer and teacher until he graduated in 1919. In 1926, he won the election for McLennan County school superintendent and then ran in 1932 for state superintendent.[37]

In October 1949, Woods published the findings from the Council of State Governments report on the status of the nations' schools, "The Forty-Eight State School Systems." The results presented a much better impression of Texas schools than reformers had led the public to believe, Woods stated. He pointed out that financial support for Texas' schools had increased from 1937–38 to 1947–48, and thirty-eight other states had more one-teacher public schools than Texas. The state ranked third in the number of teachers with degrees. Finally, the state Department of Education placed among the top ten with over 75 percent of its professional staff holding master's degrees, and among the top twelve in staff members holding PhDs.[38]

The superintendent also defended his public service record. Woods asserted that he had worked constantly for an "adequate cost-per-pupil expenditure, together with adequate training of teachers." He proclaimed, "Each two years since 1933 I have taken an oath of office pledging to enforce all existing school laws and to support our constitution," and although he opposed the Gilmer-Aikin legislation, he promised to uphold the laws of the Fifty-first Legislature. "I will exert every effort within my power to make all laws mean the most for the schools for which they were intended as long as I remain state superintendent," he declared.[39]

Woods's supporters objected to SB 115, which did away with his elected position in favor of an appointed office. As a state representative, Preston

Smith voted against the bill eliminating the elected state superintendent because he did not believe in "a central agency in the state telling the local school boards what they can or can't do."[40] Wood's assistant, W. V. Harrison of Frost, Texas, sent a diatribe against the bill to the editor of the *Dallas Morning News* alleging that it represented a betrayal of democracy:

> Our vaunted democracy is a failure. Alexander Hamilton was right in believing that the only people who can understand government, and, therefore, the only people who are qualified to conduct it, are the men who have the biggest financial stake in the commercial and industrial enterprises in the country. We may as well accept the Hamiltonian "guardianship theory" of government.
>
> What we need above everything in Texas—and it is an emergency—is a law to create a small select committee to select and appoint an expert, scholarly, high-minded set of state officials from Governor down. These appointed officials should then appoint the members of both Houses of the Legislature. We should also have educational, property, poll tax, and possibly church qualifications for voters.
>
> Our public schools have failed. They have not produced a literate citizenry capable of choosing public officials. I repent. I call upon all men everywhere in Texas to repent. What thou doest, do quickly.[41]

Some opponents threatened to challenge the Gilmer-Aikin legislation in court over the abolition of L. A. Wood's office under SB 115. Even Aikin himself admitted he did not favor an appointed superintendent.[42] Some suspected the legislation was simply a convenient way to oust Superintendent L. A. Woods, who had supported Homer Rainey's gubernatorial campaign, and who seemed to be a friend of Mexican American and African American educational opportunity.[43]

James Horany, who represented Archer City, emerged as one of the most outspoken opponents of the Gilmer-Aikin legislation in the House. "He was strong against it," Claud Gilmer remembered. "He was just one of those people that just didn't buy it," Gilmer recalled. "You couldn't criticize him. I think he was sincere." Gilmer thought that perhaps schoolteachers in Horany's district could have been loyal to Superintendent Woods, or perhaps his constituents opposed the program because of the changes that would occur in the Texas school system. Whatever reason Horany had for disliking Gilmer-Aikin, Gilmer recalled that "he opposed it and he just never did quit. I don't think he attempted to weigh it. He was just against it."[44]

Others who resisted the legislation feared an erosion of local control and an increased state presence in the schools. Superintendent L. A. Woods used this fear to oppose plans to eliminate the elected office. As he explained in a letter to Aikin, "my principals of democracy cannot allow me to take any other position than to oppose any move that tends to disfranchise the general citizenship of this State with reference to one of the most important offices within the State Government."[45]

Nevertheless, after his seventeen years in office, critics had developed a list of complaints about Woods's administration. Besides accusing the method he used to distribute Equalization funds through deputy superintendents in rural areas, who some believed used their positions to rally for Wood's campaigns, the *Dallas Morning News* reported problems between Woods's office and the state Board of Education:

> It has been part of his duties all those years to execute decisions of the State Board of Education. This co-operative relation has not been frictionless. During the last decade or so, on the contrary, it has been marked by discord between these two authorities; discord so constant as to justify saying it is chronic.[46]

If Woods was truly more inclined to favor integration, as some have suggested, it is unclear that this motivated the legislators to replace him with someone more committed to maintaining the status quo. While Woods did issue a ruling prohibiting schools from segregating Mexican American children following the Delgado case, he was only obeying the federal court's mandate. The Delgado decisions and Wood's ruling also coincided with the state's attempt to limit overt discrimination against Mexican and Mexican Americans as this had led Mexico to exclude Texas farmers from the Bracero program. Woods did have the power to suspend the accreditation of those schools that refused to comply with the Delgado ruling, and he did so in the case of Del Rio schools. One observer, however, pointed out that withdrawing accreditation held little effect. An article in the *Austin American* pointed out "that he can't legally take away per capita apportionments as a penalty. For rural aid schools lack of affiliation will mean funds for an eight month semester instead of nine months. That's the only financial threat." Students graduating from an unaccredited school would have to pass proficiency exams before entering college, but given the fact that many schools were unaccredited anyway, the effect was limited.[47] Moreover, U.S. Senator Ralph Yarborough believed Woods was simply an ineffective administrator. "He was slow to move, slow to act, slow to do anything," Yarborough remembered.[48] In the end, most reformers, business leaders, and politicians sided with Gilmer-Aikin.

The proponents carefully orchestrated the path the bills took in the House of Representatives, but opponents were also well organized. The House versions of the Gilmer- Aikin legislation was first read in the House on February 17 and referred to the Education Committee, which was chaired by Rae Files Still, so she had the power to set the agenda at a time most convenient for the bills' supporters. Because Still was one of the authors of the bills, however, propriety dictated that she step down from the chair while the bills were considered in the House, and that would leave one of the bills greatest opponents, James Horany, who was the vice chair of the Education Committee, in charge. In a carefully orchestrated display of parliamentary legerdemain, the committee instead heard the Senate version of the bills, which were facing little opposition, thus leaving Still in charge of the hearings.[49]

The House committee coordinated the public hearings with the Texas State Teachers Association, but when the hearings began on March 16, 1949, opponents were ready. The sponsors wanted to consider the bills jointly, but they failed to get the required votes. Instead, the hearings would consider the bills individually, thus stretching out the proceedings and allowing for more scrutiny. During the hearings, the bills' sponsors introduced a substantial revision of SB 115, which reorganized the state education administration. The motion to hear the bills separately was then overturned, and SB 116 and SB 117 were considered jointly. With only minor amendments to SB 116, both bills were reported favorably out of committee. The hearing ended at 5:30 A.M. on March 17, the legislature's first all-night hearing. Despite the marathon session, over 400 people reportedly packed the gallery.[50]

A rule limiting consideration on Senate bills to Wednesdays and Thursdays only, and other legislative delaying tactics, prevented the bills from being considered by the House until March 31, and then a series of amendments, discussion, and debate delayed a vote on the first measure, SB 115. Soon after the House adjourned on April 8, two representatives approached Governor Jester requesting a special session to begin in May. This development caught the legislation's supporters off guard, and they only learned about it though the news. The governor, however, announced the following Monday, April 11, that action on the legislation was of primary import to the school districts across the state, and he encouraged the House to move as quickly as possible on the measures. Opponents still conspired to delay the bill through the Easter weekend, which gave them time to orchestrate resistance to the legislation—but it also gave proponents time to plan their strategy as well. When the House reconvened on April 18, James Horany began organizing a walkout by opponents to break quorum and further delay action on Gilmer-Aikin.[51]

In this case, however, the legislation's supporters were prepared and used the walkout to their advantage. They contacted all members who supported the bills and pressed them to attend, Therefore, when the boycott occurred on April 20, only opponents were absent. When a vote revealed that the House lacked a quorum, the speaker directed the sergeant-at-arms to find and arrest absent representatives until a quorum was present, and the doorkeeper prevented anyone from leaving, effectively locking the House members in until the bill passed. Supporters then ensured they had a majority, and the bill passed 85 to 17. Possessing such a clear majority, supporters then invoked a measure rarely used in the House to suspend the requirement that the bill to be read on three separate days before the vote for final passage, and the bill passed the House.[52]

Senate Bill 116, the bill establishing the Minimum Foundation Program, was the longest of the bills, and during consideration prompted the most amendments, but considering the parliamentary acrobatics concerning SB 115, its route to approval was relatively uneventful and it passed on April 28. The finance bill, SB 117, came before the House the same day. The Gilmer-Aikin sponsors expected the bill to be approved quickly, but they were surprised when a representative offered up an amendment that was sponsored by the House speaker that would direct state funding to farm-to-market roads before funding education appropriations. The speaker explained, "People in my district are more interested in roads than in the Gilmer-Aikin program." Despite this unexpected event, the House passed the third and final Gilmer-Aikin bill that afternoon.[53]

Although bill opponents believed that the conference committee would reject most of the amendments, sponsors from both chambers accepted the amendments to SB 115 and SB 117. Only SB 116, containing the complex Minimum Foundation Program and tax formula, would be referred to a conference committee. The lieutenant governor and the speaker both named legislative sponsors to the conference committee. The committee ironed out the inconsistencies and errors in the bill, working for most of the month of May. The conference report was approved in the Senate on May 31 and in the House on June 1. Governor Jester signed SB 115 on June 1 and SB 116 and SB 117 on June 8. Voters elected members of the state Board of Education on November 8, 1949. In February 1950, after a six-week search, the board appointed J. W. Edgar the new commissioner of education. Edgar was the former superintendent of the Orange and later Austin school districts. L. A. Woods served as a consultant until the end his term at the close of 1950.[54]

Gov. Beauford H. Jester signs SB 116. Behind Governor Jester, left to right: Longview school superintendent Henry L. Foster, Rep. Dolph Briscoe, Jr. (Uvalde), Rep. George O. Nokes, Jr. (Corsicana), former Sen. James E. Taylor (Kerens), Rep. Rae Files Still (Waxahachie), Texas State Teachers Association public relations director Charles Tennyson, former Rep. Claud H. Gilmer (Rocksprings), Rep. Jim T. Lindsey (Boston), Rep. T. Durwood Manford (Smiley), Sen. Ottis E. Lock (Lufkin), Lt. Gov. Alan Shivers, Sen. A. M. Aikin Jr. (Paris), Sen. George C. Morris (Greenville), Sen. Robert L. Proffer (Dustin). Photograph by Neal Douglass, PICA ND-49-A020-02 Austin History Center, Austin Public Library.

*Chapter 6*

# Epilogue

Although opponents of the Gilmer-Aikin legislation worried that the bill would erode democracy, increase spending, and destroy the rural community, the new program garnered praise from all areas. For school districts in poor areas, Gilmer-Aikin meant more funds to improve local schools.

## PUBLIC SUPPORT FOR THE GILMER-AIKIN BILLS

Irvin Wilson, superintendent of schools in Hallsville, in Harrison County, Texas, wrote to Senator Aikin about the need for funding in his district. "We have 500 students," Wilson noted, "and do not even have a gymnasium." The school also needed money to repair its buses. He concluded, "The people as a whole want this thing done. They are hoping the legislature will do this." If the Gilmer-Aikin legislation needed support, Wilson would come to Austin. "If necessary, I could bring the county board, county superintendents, and other school men down there," he offered.[1] The groundswell of general interest in the legislation surprised even veteran Austin observers. An editorial in the *Austin American* in early May 1949 acknowledged the influence of public opinion on the legislature. "Lobbying has become the people's business," it noted. Political persuasion was once the purview of former senators and representatives and professional lobbyists, but now public citizens began to exert pressure on the Fifty-first Legislature. The writer guessed three times as many Texans came to Austin to speak their mind on legislation—some 3,000 interested people, many of them teachers. The shift from professional lobbyists to concerned citizens seemed a positive step, the writer concluded. In her history of the legislative battle, Rep. Rae Files Still of Waxahachie noted,

"House members complained daily about the increased burden placed on them" by the number of calls, letters, telegrams, and personal visits regarding the pending legislation.[2] The education reporter for the *Dallas Morning News,* Alonzo Wasson, reported:

> The people of Texas have learned, or at least are beginning to learn, the improvidence of the small school. They have, for example, reduced the number of common school districts in this state from something more than 7,000 (100 in a single county at one time) to about half that number. But it has taken them twenty or thirty years to accomplish that reform.[3]

Much of the public support came from rural areas, and this influenced rural representatives to support the reforms. Just as Claud Gilmer believed his education limited his opportunities, A. M. Aikin remembered of his own schooling:

> I studied physics in a country school where we didn't have anything but a book—no laboratory facilities of any kind, not even a sink. I came here thinking a child ought to get an equal educational opportunity whether he was born in an oil field or a cotton patch. That was the underlying principal of the Gilmer-Aikin program. I still believe that.[4]

## REACTION TO THE GILMER-AIKIN LAWS

Letters of approval flooded in from across the state: "It is possible that in the coming years the [Gilmer-Aikin legislation] will be considered as the greatest single step forward in the history of Texas public education. Millions of Texas school children will doubtless profit because of this legislation."[5] Another praised the bills saying, "Surely this is our best investment in democracy."[6] One predicted "that the people of Texas shall always be grateful to you for your part in improving the educational opportunities for their children."[7] Another proclaimed Gilmer-Aikin the "most progressive and far reaching measures that the legislature has yet passed" and correctly predicted that Aikin's name would be forever associated with the legislation.[8] A writer reflected with state pride, "I feel that the Minimum Foundation Program will be the starting point of making Texas schools the envy of the rest of the nation," and praised Aikin's long hours of work in support of the bills.[9]

The Avery Independent School District superintendent, Frank C. Bean, wrote praising Aikin's support of rural education: "We teachers will always feel that your fight to enlighten the governor played a major roll [*sic*] in getting our MAGNA CHARTA." Bean then offered Aikin the appreciation of the entire school district stating, "Every teacher I know has the very highest regard for you, and aside from any personal feelings that I may have, I am looking forward to your progress in any field you choose."[10]

The conflict between Aikin and Woods exemplified the debate over school reform. Both had been rural schoolteachers in East Texas. Both had seen the strengths and weaknesses of rural schools. Woods had been a progressive educator, but his progressivism reflected an earlier generation. Woods based his progressivism on the earlier belief that improving the country schools would improve rural life, and he wanted to preserve rural schools. Furthermore, he believed the role of a superintendent should be to formulate change slowly. As a 1912 report on rural education stated, "Educational revolutions sometimes revolve backward. Evolution is better and safer."[11]

But the reform Aikin endorsed represented a new rural progressivism. This was a reform movement that favored increased efficiency. "There is only one goal and only one to be considered and that is do we get a better school system or not. The real reason for working on these bills is to try to get a better school system."[12] Former governor Dolph Briscoe, who was a freshman legislator during the Gilmer-Aikin legislative hearings, described the educational reform as nothing short of as revolutionary. "Revolutionary is a strong word, but I don't know any other term that so accurately fits that time and place in our educational history," he stated.[13]

After Gov. Allan Shivers signed Gilmer-Aikin, the *Texas Outlook* proclaimed it "One of the greatest chapters in the history of the Texas State Teachers Association has just been written." The legislation immediately made its impact felt across the state. The principal of a Lubbock school wrote A. M. Aikin, "Your efforts in behalf of education in Texas are already beginning to pay dividends." She noted guardedly, "the quality of teachers has improved somewhat." But she stated optimistically, "Now that you have given us a really good bill, I feel that the next few years should show a definite improvement." She thanked Aikin for his efforts and promised that educators would do the same. "You have made a most generous contribution to education. In return, we are going to try to give a full dollar's worth of service for every dollar you have given us."[14]

Gilmer-Aikin originated as a means of increasing salaries for Texas schoolteachers. As part of a nationwide call for higher salaries for educators in the wake of World War II, the laws served their purpose. Yet for Texas history, Gilmer-Aikin represented much more than a simple pay raise. It also represented a reaction to the changes in the nation and Texas following World War II. After the war, reformers took advantage of changes in the Texas economy and society to press for legislation so schools could adapt to those changes. The enactment increased minority enrollment, funds for libraries, the number of public school teachers, and services for disabled students. Another important result of the laws came in changing public emphasis from the importance of "localism" and "regionalism" in educational control to the need for a "national" system of education. Finally, Gilmer-Aikin signaled another step toward the goal of democratizing education.

A salary increase for public school teachers was the immediate benefit of Gilmer-Aikin. In West Texas, one African American teacher said:

> The biggest change that I noticed was the salary. Because, see, my father made as little as seventy-five dollars a month teaching and working seven months out of the year. And he had to do other things to maintain his family during the five months that he didn't teach. And he also went to school. Then when he came to Slaton, he made a big increase in salary from seventy-five dollars to ninety dollars a month. And when I finished my first job under Gilmer-Aikin, I made $2,405 a year, and that was a fantastic salary. Of course, he benefited from it, too. He just thought it was fantastic.[15]

While the acts significantly increased salaries for black teachers, a white teacher complained that the pay raises were still not high enough. She received $208 per month, but her necessary monthly expenses ran $215 per month. While she admitted the raises helped, "The thing I'm trying to emphasize is that teachers have been thrown a bone, and many of them seem perfectly satisfied." School superintendents believed that the increases in the teachers' salaries were adequate to retain qualified teachers. Most African American teachers considered the salary equalization a blessing.[16]

Moreover, the new teachers' pay scale encouraged further professional training and higher degrees. Registrars at many Texas universities noted an increased number of students enrolled in teacher-training programs. In 1950, schools hired two thousand new teachers, with plans to hire another 1,500 the next year. The Minimum Foundation Program also provided funding for small districts that often suffered from staffing shortages to pool their resources to hire at least one full-time supervisor, counselor, librarian, school nurse, physician, or temporary teachers to serve several districts. Even if Gilmer-Aikin did not fix the entire teacher shortage problem, they did help the overall situation.[17]

World War II demonstrated that the nation's schools needed continued reform. The Gilmer-Aikin program did more than simply bring Texas schools into the twentieth century. The program provided more funds, a more efficient state school system, and expanded services to students. As the baby boom increased the scholastic population, the number and types of classes increased, as did libraries, infirmaries, and vocational education shops. To staff the expanded classes, schools needed to hire an increasing number of better-trained and better-paid teachers and support personnel.

In 1948, Texas had a school-age (six to seventeen) population of 1.5 million children, and another 1 million under the age of six. Estimates predicted that these children would translate into a net increase of 40,000 new school-age children annually. Educators predicted the increases would continue throughout the decade and eventually affect the number of students enrolling in the state's colleges and universities.[18]

The large Houston Independent School District announced that in the 1949–50 school year it would undertake a building program to accommodate the increasing number of children in the urban district. Superintendent William E. Moreland also noted that Houston schools would expand their vocational education programs, reading clinics, and health programs. The Gilmer-Aikin Laws allocated funds so smaller school districts could also enhance their programs. The rural Kerrville Independent School District expanded its health program because of Gilmer-Aikin, "and the result was a well-equipped and well-run clinic in each school."[19]

Gilmer-Aikin provided more funds for schoolchildren who traditionally had received only a limited education. By doing so, the laws created a greater possibility of increased educational opportunity for all Texas schoolchildren. An editorial in the *Texas Outlook* reminded readers that unequal distribution of the equalization funding had been one of the criticisms against the old system that Gilmer-Aikin sought to correct. Even before the Depression, "American public education was not a single system with 145,000 local branches but rather a spectrum from affluence to shocking scarcity." "One thing that we should keep in mind is that the schools are for the benefit of the school children of Texas, not for the convenience of teachers, administrators, and school boards" the author said. "A bill that is introduced must be for the entire state—for every child—and not for certain sections and certain groups of children."[20]

Yale sociologist Burton R. Clark wrote that before World War II, education remained a local issue. "The federal government only occasionally concerned itself with education." Americans perceived no need for a national education standard:

> At the local and state levels, concern was often intense, but still education was not seen as so crucial to the well-being of society as to promote a sense of large crisis, to command the sustained attention of public officials and the general public, and to generate the dogged will and the special programs to correct its errors. After all, the raising of the young would still be mainly in the hands of the family, church, and community. Men could still make it without extensive formal schooling; the image of the self-made man on the frontier, in industry, and in commerce still loomed large in the American mind. If there was such a thing as an educational column, or even 'educational news,' in the newspaper, it was back somewhere around the want ads.[21]

World War II challenged Americans to see education not as a privilege but as an essential element in preserving democracy.

Whether they had been students in rural areas, minority students, or students with medical or physical limitations, the high number of draftees rejected by the military drew attention to the disadvantages many school children faced. The embarrassment this brought to Texas education caused lawmakers to increase standardization and lessen the educational disadvantage children encountered. Improvements following Gilmer-Aikin included a 50 percent increase in classes for handicapped children and 600 new vocational education classes. There were more minority students attending classes and there was a 5 percent increase statewide in African American and Mexican American attendance—as much as a 15 percent increase in some areas. Apportioning funds according to average daily attendance and a natural increase caused by the baby boom probably contributed to the increased attendance statistics.[22]

The increased opportunity reflected a growing call for democratization in U.S. and Texas education. Ironically, a few years later some anti-integrationists tried to use Gilmer-Aikin to oppose the *Brown* decision in 1954. In 1955, the Texas Citizens Council tried unsuccessfully to prevent the integration of the Big Spring Independent School District and deny state funding to schools that did integrate because Gilmer-Aikin stipulated that school funds be distributed on a separate basis.[23]

Despite its benefits, Gilmer-Aikin did not solve all Texas public education problems. Some small, underfinanced rural schools still suffered from overworked teachers and poor attendance: "There is evidence of dynamic

leadership in certain county units, but on the whole the supervisory activities, while generally helpful, have been haphazard and piecemeal rather than
systematically conceived and developed." This seemed to be a condemnation
of the methods of administration of rural schools in general, more than a
criticism of the changes wrought by Gilmer-Aikin.[24]

When the 1948 Governors' Conference called for a report on state educational systems in the United States, the report described the current method
states used to finance their public school systems as "obsolete and inequitable." Gilmer-Aikin aligned the Texas school system with recommendations in the report. For example, the commissioner—who had replaced the
superintendent—had become an appointed position rather than elected and
could order statewide educational reports and studies. The Chief Educational Authority, made up of the commissioner, the state Board of Education,
and the state Department of Education, fulfilled the suggestion for a state
policy-making agency. Texas consolidated smaller school districts, cutting the
number of districts almost in half, from over 4,000 to just over 2,000. The
idea of consolidating school districts in the name of efficiency continued to
upset some local citizens not only in Texas but also in areas considered more
educationally advanced. As late as 1957, attempts to consolidate some of the
fifty-four districts in Bergen County, New Jersey, met fierce opposition from
local communities.[25]

In a state unused to providing much money to public education, some
believed that Gilmer-Aikin provided schools "more than their fair share of
the state tax dollar." The program cost the state $135 million per year, $30
million more than in previous years. Yet, supporters pointed out that the
legislature assumed that it would cost the state at least $30 million more
with increased teachers salaries, not taking into account other school improvements.[26] Although Texas almost tripled the amount of money it spent
on education from 1938 to 1948, the increase proved misleading because of
inflation. Compared to Texans' personal income, the amount dedicated to
educating Texas children actually had dropped from 1937 to 1948. Supporters
maintained that Gilmer-Aikin "restored public education to the position in
the total state finance picture that it held 10 years ago."[27] They also argued
the costs of better education would eventually pay for themselves because
better-educated students would not become wards of the state. One article
pointed out the low educational levels of prison inmates and suggested that
by providing better education the state would have fewer criminals.[28]

To counter opposition to the reform changes, the Texas State Teachers

Association insisted that "teachers have an obligation to become literate in school finance."[29] The *Texas Outlook* reinforced this by listing several reasons why teachers should stay informed:

> If questioned on the necessity of educational costs teachers should respond that education is necessary for democracy and needs support; teachers should familiarize themselves with the governmental process in order to prevent waste and inefficiency; educators should be aware that school budgets are sometimes tied to other issues therefore care must be taken to vote on the merits of education.[30]

Besides providing necessary information to encourage public support for increased educational funding, teachers needed to stress the importance of efficiency and accountability in public education. Small schools were "inefficient and poorly organized and therefore cost-ineffective." With these reminders, the TSTA hoped that its members would support education finance bills at the local level and encourage parents to support Gilmer-Aikin. The classroom teacher had the power to persuade and inform the voters of the benefits of school reform, because, the *Texas Outlook* explained, "People always are against what they do not understand; so it is up to us to meet with them and talk frankly about the proposals."[31]

In the half century and more since the Texas legislature passed Gilmer-Aikin, the importance of public schools has become something that classroom teachers no longer need to emphasize to parents. In fact, within less than a decade after Gilmer-Aikin, Texas public schools faced two monumental challenges. The first came in 1954 with the Supreme Court's decision to strike down segregation with the *Brown* case. The second came three years later when the Soviet Union, the United States' cold war nemesis, trumpeted its technological superiority with the launch and orbit of *Sputnik I*. In both cases the challenge to public education was not local or regional, but national in scope. Solutions to perceived weaknesses in public education became a nationwide concern in the 1950s. During the 1960s, former Texas teacher Lyndon Johnson became president and encouraged congressional passage of over sixty educational bills, earning him the title "The Education President." Later, Pres. George W. Bush, another Texan, also stressed the importance of public school improvement. Far from being an issue that the public often ignored, public education became a critical issue in the years after World War II.

Gilmer-Aikin did much more than update the Texas educational system. The bills were part of a national trend to standardize and democratize
public education. During and after World War II, Americans in general believed that education was important to democracy, but the war revealed that
public schools were not graduating students ready to come to the assistance
of their country—instead they were unprepared and unhealthy. Across the
region, southern states began to centralize their public school systems and
call attention to the need for greater efficiency than was possible in rural one-
room schools.

At the same time, the regional effort by the NAACP to equalize teachers' salaries for African American instructors with their white counterparts
illustrates best the changing racial attitudes in the southern states following
World War II that influenced the Gilmer-Aikin legislation. The combination
of professional educators calling attention to the necessity of educational
opportunity for minority children in the South, and the legal struggle these
groups initiated themselves, challenged the states to provide better schools
for African Americans and Mexican Americans in Texas. And because poor
white children increasingly attended inadequately funded rural schools before and during the Depression, they benefited as well.

Finally, although the influences behind the public school reforms were
not unique to Texas, Gilmer-Aikin did point to two significant developments
in Texas history. First, the state's rural communities and their legislative representatives understood the trend toward urbanization following World War II
and encouraged preserving rural schools through improvement and consolidation. Concomitantly, improvements in rural roads and transportation encouraged consolidation by making it easier for rural children to travel greater
distances to attend school. Second, the years following World War II were the
first time Texas lawmakers had any real money to distribute to public schools.
Although influential Texans from Stephen F. Austin onward espoused the
idea of free education, the state lacked the funds and organizational infrastructure to establish a system of public schools. In 1854, the state began
to play a role in supporting free schools, but the state's contribution only
supplemented local funds until after the war effort relieved the effects of the
Depression for the nation and the state.

The Gilmer-Aikin legislation signaled an effort to align the state's public
schools with regional and national educational trends and reflected the increased value Texans could afford to place on education after World War II.
Certainly, Gilmer-Aikin did not solve every problem that Texas public schools

faced. In the early twenty-first century, questions over tax limits, equal distribution of school funds, the role of the state in public education, teacher
training and salaries, curriculum standardization, and central versus local
authority continue to confound Texas lawmakers and their constituents—
and will as long as citizens are concerned about children's education.

In the Texas State Capitol Complex, beneath the main floor and near the
Capitol lunchroom is a pantheon of Texas political leaders. The bronze busts
of Gib Lewis, Lyndon Johnson, and others form a half circle of some of the
most important Texas politicians. At the very end is a glistening bronze bust
of a small, bespectacled man named A. M. Aikin Jr. Over a generation after
his death, the name A. M. Aikin may not be as familiar as it once was, yet it
is preserved in the names of elementary schools, scholarships, and endowed
chairs of education.[32]

A. M. Aikin retired in 1979, after having represented the people of East
Texas for forty-six years. During that tenure he only missed two and a half
days and was named "Dean of the Texas Senate." He had been chairman of
the powerful Senate Finance Committee from 1967 until he retired, and he
became known as the "Father of Modern Texas Education" because of his
long endorsement of state public schools. Between the years 1937 and 1965
alone, he either sponsored or directed nearly 150 education bills. His commitment to educating all Texas school children lasted until his final years.
When Paris Junior College named its science building in his honor, he re-
marked, "Until all young Texans have the more or less equal chance to show
their skills and develop their talents, whether black or Mexican American or
white Anglo, we won't have finished the long road that our forefathers set
before us."[33]

Gilmer-Aikin, more than any other legislation, bound A. M. Aikin's
name to the issue of Texas public school reform. The Fifty-first Legislature
passed three laws in 1949 completely reorganizing the state's public school
system and signaling the most significant turning point in Texas educational
history in the twentieth century. The new laws replaced the elected office of
state superintendent with an appointed commissioner, raised teachers' salaries without regard to sex or race, expanded the role of the state in what had
been a local responsibility, and increased the amount of money the state spent
on education. The new legislation also accelerated the end of the one-room
school and paved the way for rural school consolidation.

While some later looked back at the legacy of the one-room school with
sentimentality, Gilmer-Aikin made it possible for future generations of stu-

dents to have better educational opportunities than Aikin and his fellow legislators had. In the end, perhaps, the grandest honor befitting those who worked so tirelessly on behalf of Texas education is not a bronze bust in the Capitol building, but the thousands of Texas high school students who graduate each year from accredited high schools.

# NOTES

## INTRODUCTION

1. B. F. Pittenger, "Annie Webb Blanton," *Texas Outlook,* January 1946, 19.

2. "Resolutions Passed by House of Delegates," *Texas Outlook,* January 1946, 22.

3. Chas. H. Tennyson, "How They Became Law," *Texas Outlook,* August 1950, 18.

4. Robert A. Calvert and Arnoldo De León, *The History of Texas,* 2nd ed. (Wheeling, Ill.: Harlan Davidson, 1996), 354.

5. Lawrence A. Cremin, *The Transformation of the School: Progressivism in American Education, 1876–1957* (New York: Alfred A. Knopf, 1961).

6. David B. Tyack, *The One Best System: A History of American Urban Education* (Cambridge, Mass.: Harvard University Press, 1974); William A. Link, *A Hard Country and a Lonely Place: Schooling, Society, and Reform in Rural Virginia, 1870–1920* (Chapel Hill: University of North Carolina Press, 1986); William A. Link, *The Paradox of Southern Progressivism, 1880–1930* (Chapel Hill: University of North Carolina Press, 1992); Diane Ravitch, *Left Back: A Century of Battles Over School Reform* (New York: Simon & Schuster, 2000).

7. Fredrick Eby, *Education in Texas* (Austin: The University of Texas Press, 1925); C. E. Evans, *The Story of Texas Schools* (Austin, Tex.: The Steck Company, 1955); Thad Stitton and Milam C. Rowold, *Ringing the Children In: Texas Country Schools* (College Station: Texas A&M University Press, 1987); Luther Bryan Clegg, ed., *The Empty Schoolhouse: Memories of One-Room Texas Schools* (College Station: Texas A&M University Press, 1997); Guadalupe San Miguel Jr., *"Let All of Them Take Heed": Mexican American and the Campaign for Educational Equality in Texas, 1910–1981* (Austin: University of Texas Press, 1987), and *Brown, Not White: School Integration and the Chicano Movement in Houston* (College Station: Texas A&M University Press, 2001); Robyn Duff Landino, *Desegregating Texas Schools: Eisenhower, Shivers, and the Crisis at Mansfield High* (Austin: University of Texas Press, 1996); William Henry Kellar, *Make Haste Slowly: Moderates, Conservatives, and School Desegregation in Houston* (College Station: Texas A&M University Press, 1999); Carlos Kevin Blanton, *The Strange Career of Bilingual Education in Texas, 1836–1981* (College Station: Texas A&M University Press, 2004).

8. Rae Files Still, *The Gilmer-Aikin Bills: A Study in the Legislative Process* (Austin, Tex.: The Steck Company, 1950).

9. George Norris Green, *The Establishment in Texas Politics: The Primitive Years, 1938–1957* (Norman: University of Oklahoma Press, 1979).

## CHAPTER I

1. Mattie Austin Hatcher, "Plan of Stephen F. Austin for an Institute of Modern Languages at San Felipe de Austin," *Texas Historical Association Quarterly* 12 (January 1909): 231.

2. William Ransom Hogan, *The Texas Republic: A Social and Economic History* (Austin: University of Texas Press, 1969), 136.

3. Evans, 52.

4. *Texas Constitution* (1845), art. 10, sec. 1, in *Documents of Texas History,* 2nd ed., eds. Ernest Wallace, David M. Vigness, and George B. Ward. (Austin: Texas State Historical Association, 2002) reprinted from United States, 29th Cong., 1st sess., *House Executive Documents,* No. 16 (Washington, D.C., 1845), 2–22.

5. "Boundary of Texas, Territory of New Mexico," September 9, 1850, *Statutes at Large and Treaties* 9 (December 1845–March 1851), 446.

6. Alton Hornsby Jr., "The Freedmen's Bureau Schools in Texas, 1865–1870," *Southwestern Historical Quarterly* 76 (April 1973): 397–417; Barry A. Crouch, *The Freedmen's Bureau and Black Texans* (Austin: University of Texas Press, 1992), 19; Claude Elliott, "The Freedmen's Bureau in Texas," *Southwestern Historical Quarterly* 56 (July 1952): 1–24.

7. John H. Reagan, *Memoirs* (New York: Neal, 1906), 286–295, in Wallace, *Documents in Texas History,* 203.

8. Ann Patton Baenziger, "Bold Beginnings: The Radical Program in Texas, 1870–1873" (Master's thesis, Southwest Texas State University, 1970); W. C. Nunn, *Texas Under the Carpetbaggers* (Austin: University of Texas Press, 1962); Carl H. Moneyhon, "Public Education and Texas Reconstruction," *Southwestern Historical Quarterly* 92 (January 1989); and James M. Smallwood, *Time of Hope, Time of Despair: Black Texans During Reconstruction,* Series in Ethnic Studies (Port Washington, N.Y.: Kennikat Press, 1981); Eby, *Education in Texas,* 157.

9. Alwyn Barr, *Black Texans: A History of African Americans in Texas, 1528–1995* (Norman: University of Oklahoma Press, 1996), 23; Randolph B. Campbell, *An Empire for Slavery: The Peculiar Institution in Texas, 1821–1865* (Baton Rouge: Louisiana State University Press, 1989), 175–76; Hornsby, "Freedmen's Bureau Schools," 398; Barry A. Crouch, "A Spirit of Lawlessness: White Violence; Texas Blacks, 1865–1868," *Journal of Social History* 18 (Winter 1984): 225; James M. Smallwood, *The Feud That Wasn't: The Taylor Ring, Bill Sutton, John Wesley Hardin, and Violence in Texas* (College Station: Texas A&M University Press, 2008), 16.

10. *Laws of Texas* 8 (15th Leg., 1871, C. S.), 113–118; J. L. M. Curry, *A Brief Sketch of George Peabody, and a History of the Peabody Education Fund Through Thirty Years* (1898; reprint, New York: Negro University Press, 1969), 58; Walace Hawkins, "Col. Jacob Carl DeGress," Walace Hawkins Literary Effort, Archive and Information Services Division, Texas State Library and Archive Commission, Austin, Texas, 48; Carl H. Moneyhon, "Public Education and Texas Reconstruction Politics, 1871–1874," *Southwestern Historical Quarterly* 92 (January 1989): 395.

11. Hawkins, 8–45.

12. Ibid., 45–58; Tax-Payers' Convention of the State of Texas, *Proceedings of the Tax-Payers' Convention of the State of Texas* (Galveston, Tex.: News Steam Book and Job Office, 1871), 17.

13. Hawkins, 45–68; Moneyhon, "Public Education and Texas Reconstruction Politics," 397–416; Campbell, *Gone to Texas,* 282–83.

14. *Texas Constitution,* art. 7, sec. 3; *Laws of Texas* 8 (15th Leg., 1876), 199–210; Patrick G. Williams, *Beyond Redemption: Texas Democrats After Reconstruction* (College Station: Texas A&M University Press, 2007), 122–25.

15. *Handbook of Texas Online,* s.v. "Rufus Columbus Burleson," http://www.tshaonline .org/handbook/online/articles/BB/fbu44.html (accessed on June 1, 2008); Campbell, *Gone to Texas,* 317–18; Rupert N. Richardson, et al., *Texas: The Lone Star State,* 9th ed. (Upper Saddle River, N.J.: Pearson Prentice Hall, 2005), 247; *Handbook of Texas Online,* s.v. "Oran Milo Roberts," http://www.tshaonline.org/handbook/online/articles/RR/fro18.html (accessed on June 1, 2008); Alwyn Barr, *Reconstruction to Reform: Texas Politics, 1876–1906* (1971; reprint, Dallas: Southern Methodist University Press, 2000), 79; Williams, *Beyond Redemption,* 125, 148, 151–54.

16. Mindy Spearman, "'Everything to Help, Nothing to Hinder': The Story of the *Texas School Journal*," *Southwestern Historical Quarterly* III (January 2008): 283, 286–7; *Laws of Texas* 9 (18th Leg., R.S., 1883), 134; *Laws of Texas* 9 (18th Leg., S.S., 1884), 38–56; Williams, *Beyond Redemption*, 161–62.

17. C. Vann Woodward, *Origins of the New South, 1877–1913* (Baton Rouge: Louisiana State University Press, 1951), 398.

18. Ibid., 398–99.

19. James A. Tinsley, "The Progressive Movement in Texas," (PhD diss., University of Wisconsin, 1953), 175.

20. Eby, 232–33, 216–17; Williams, *Beyond Redemption*, 164.

21. Eby, 232–33, 216–17.

22. Ibid., 216–17. In 1900, the reported assessed value of school property in towns was worth almost twice that of rural schools, $5,046,461 compared to $2,648,180.


## CHAPTER 2


1. Clegg, 8.

2. Ibid., 9.

3. Ibid.

4. Tinsley, 10–11.

5. Arthur S. Link, "What Happened to the Progressive Movement in the 1920's?" *American Historical Review* 64 (July 1959): 8367; David B. Danbom, *"The World of Hope": Progressives and the Struggle for an Ethical Public Life* (Philadelphia: Temple University Press, 1987), viii.

6. Dewey W. Grantham Jr., "The Contours of Southern Progressivism," *American Historical Review* 86 (1981): 1036, 1045; Dewey W. Grantham Jr., *Southern Progressivism: The Reconciliation of Progress and Tradition* (Knoxville: The University of Tennessee Press, 1983), 1.

7. Don H. Doyle, *New Men, New Cities, New South: Atlanta, Nashville, Charleston, Mobile, 1860–1910* (Chapel Hill: University of North Carolina Press, 1990), 148; Paul M. Gaston, *The New South Creed: A Study in Southern Mythmaking* (New York: Alfred A. Knopf, 1970), 103–5.

8. Grantham, "Contours," 1044–45.

9. Edwin Mims, "The South Realizing Itself: Redeemers of the Soil," *World's Work* 23 (November 1911): 54; C. Vann Woodward, *Origins of the New South, 1877–1913* (Baton Rouge: Louisiana State University Press, 1951), 397.

10. Arthur S. Link, "The Progressive Movement in the South, 1870–1914," *North Carolina Historical Review* 23 (April 1946): 172, 178–79; Grantham, "Contours," 1050; Tinsley, 1.

11. Dewey W. Grantham Jr., "Texas Congressional Leaders and the New Freedom, 1913–1917," *Southwestern Historical Quarterly* 53 (July 1949): 35.

12. Link, "What Happened," 838–39, 845, 849; George Brown Tindall, *The Emergence of the New South* (Baton Rouge: Louisiana State University Press, 1967), 219; Tinsley, "Progressive Movement," 180.

13. Edwin Mims, "The South Realizing Itself: Remakers of Industry," *World's Work* 23 (December 1911): 203, 217; Tindall, *Emergence of the New South*, 232; Mims, "Redeemers of the Soil," 50; Link, "Progressive Movement in the South," 174–76; Grantham, "Contours," 1049–50.

14. Mims, "Remakers of Industry," 216; Woodward, 398.

15. W. H. Heck, "The Educational Uplift in the South," *World's Work* 8 (1904): 5027.

16. Tindall, 223–24; Grantham, "Contours," 1048–50; See also W. H. Heck, 5029, and John Spencer Bassett, "How Industrialism Builds Up Education," *World's Work* 8 (1904): 5031; James D. Anderson, *The Education of Blacks in the South, 1860–1935* (Chapel Hill: University of North Carolina Press, 1988), 81.

17. Holland Thompson, "Some Effects of Industrialism in an Agricultural State," *South Atlantic Quarterly* 4 (January 1905): 74.

18. H. E. Singleton, "Annual Address of the President," in *Proceedings of the Eighteenth Annual Session of the Texas Farmers' Congress in College Station, Texas, August 2–4, 1915* (Austin, Tex.: Von Boeckmann-Jones Co., 1916), 12.

19. Richard Hofstadter, *The Age of Reform: From Bryan to F. D. R.* (New York: Alfred A. Knopf, 1955; Vintage Books, 1960), chapter 1; Cremin, *Transformation of the School,* 41–50, 75–85; David B. Tyack, *The One Best System: A History of American Urban Education* (Cambridge, Mass.: Harvard University Press, 1974); 23; David B. Danbom, *Born in the Country: A History of Rural America* (Baltimore: Johns Hopkins University Press, 1995), 167–75.

20. Singleton, 13.

21. Frederick T. Gates, "The Country School of To-Morrow," *World's Work* 24 (August 1912): 460–66.

22. Ibid., 462–63.

23. Ibid., 464–66; Tyack, *One Best System,* 23.

24. Cremin, *Transformation of the School,* vii–ix.

25. Grantham, "Contours," 1047; Eby, *Education in Texas,* 216.

26. Link, "Progressive Movement in the South," 172; Lewis L. Gould, *Progressives and Prohibitionists: Texas Democrats in the Wilson Era* (Austin: University of Texas Press, 1973) xii; Richard Hofstadter, ed., *The Progressive Movement* (Englewood Cliffs, N.J.: Prentice Hall, 1963), 1–3; William A. Link, *The Paradox of Southern Progressivism, 1880–1930* (Chapel Hill: University of North Carolina Press, 1992), 131.

27. Evans, 115.

28. Ibid., 115–116; *Texas Laws* 14 (31st Leg., R.S., 1909), sec. 154, 21; sec 77, 20; sec 57, 18.

29. *Texas Laws* 13 (30th Leg., 1st C.S.), sec. 1, 231; *Texas Laws* 19 (36th Leg., R.S., 1919), 41–47; *Texas Laws* 22 (39th Leg., R.S., 1925), sec. 5, 420; *Texas Laws* 26 (41st Leg., 1st C.S., 1929), sec. 5(e), 88.

30. *Texas Laws* 15 (32nd Leg., 1st C.S., 1911), 74–76; *Texas Laws* 15 (32nd Leg., R.S., 1911), sec. 3–5, 35–36; *Texas Laws* 18 (35th Leg., R.S., 1917), sec. 4, 152–53; *Texas Laws* 26 (41st Leg., 1st C.S., 1929), 86–90.

31. Eby, 127, 230–31; *Texas Laws* 17 (34th Leg., R.S., 1915), sec. 1–2, 93.

32. *Texas Laws* 15 (32nd Leg., R.S., 1911), sec. 3, 35.

33. Debbie Mauldin Cottrell, *Pioneer Woman Educator: The Progressive Spirit of Annie Webb Blanton* (College Station: Texas A&M University Press, 1993), 67–68.

34. In Evans, 125.

35. *Texas Laws* 19 (36th Leg., R.S., 1919), sec. 1–2, 356–57.

36. Genevieve Smith, "The Junior Schools of San Antonio," *Texas Outlook,* November 1924, 10.

37. Danbom, *World of Hope,* 120–21; Raymond E. Callahan, *Education and the Cult of Efficiency: A Study of the Social Forces That Have Shaped the Administration of the Public Schools* (Chicago: University of Chicago Press, 1962): 5–6; David Tyack, Robert Lowe, and Elisabeth Hansot, *Public Schools in Hard Times: The Great Depression and Recent Years* (Cambridge, Mass.: Harvard University Press, 1984), 21.

38. Diane Ravitch, *Left Back: A Century of Battles Over School Reform* (New York: Simon & Schuster, 2000), 102–4; David Tyack and Elisabeth Hansot, *Managers of Virtue: Public School Leadership in America, 1820–1980* (New York: Basic Books, 1982), 161.

39. W. Lee O'Daniel, Speech of October 15, 1939, transcript, Governor W. Lee O'Daniel Papers, Texas State Library and Archive, Austin, Texas, 2.

40. Seth Shepard McKay, *W. Lee O'Daniel and Texas Politics, 1938–1942* (Lubbock: Texas Tech Press, 1944), 328, 105; M. Scott Sosebee, "The Split in the Texas Democratic Party, 1936–1956," (Master's thesis, Texas Tech University, 2000), 29–30.

41. McKay, *O'Daniel,* 127.

42. Ibid., 327; Lady Bird Johnson, *The American Experience, LBJ,* "Part 1-Beautiful Texas," written and produced by Dave Grubin, 60 min., North Texas Public Broadcasting, Inc., 1991, videocassette; McKay, *O'Daniel,* 345–46.

43. Speaker Claud Gilmer to Corrinne E. Crow, November 15, 1976, Aikin Special Project, East Texas State University Oral History Program, James G. Gee Library, Texas A&M University–Commerce, 51–52. (Hereafter cited as Aikin Oral History Project.)

44. Texas State Board of Education, *Report on the Results of the Texas Statewide School Adequacy Survey* (Austin: Texas State Board of Education, 1937). This report was based upon the findings of the Works Progress Administration Official Project 66-66-7752, approved by Franklin Roosevelt on February 6, 1935. According to the forward, the project was a "statistical and research study of the Texas Public School situation with particular attention to be paid to the efficiency of the existing organization of administrative units, adequacy of public school plants, and the problem of sources and adequacy of amounts of school support with possibility of more equitable distribution of state school monies." The findings were to be turned over to the state legislature, which in turn would pass legislation to remedy any findings of inequality in funding.

45. O'Daniel, transcript, 2.

46. Ibid., 3.

47. Ibid.

48. Ibid., 4–5.

49. Ibid., 5–6.

50. Ibid., 5, 9.

51. H. W. Stilwell, draft letter to the Members of the Governor's Educational Commission, October 30, 1940, Governor W. Lee O'Daniel Papers, Texas State Library and Archive, Austin, Texas (hereafter O'Daniel Papers).

52. John T. Boydaton, J. D. Travis, and Rube Gray, letter to Governor O'Daniel, February 27, 1941, O'Daniel Papers.

53. Editorial, *Fort Worth Press,* November 28, 1940.

54. L. A. Woods, *Thirty-First Biennial Report, State Department of Education 1938–1939 and 1939–1940,* December 1940, "Recommendations," O'Daniel Papers, 2.

55. "Texas Schools Rank 25th in Nation," *Dallas Morning News,* December 14, 1940, 13I; John Wagner, "Board Divides on O'Daniel's School Plan," *Dallas Morning News,* December 19, 1940, 7I.

56. W. L. Hughes, "Our Major Educational Problems," *Texas Outlook,* February 1940, 36–38.

57. John K. Norton, "The Myth of Educational Equality," *American Mercury,* January 1946, 17; L. D. Stokes, "Inequalities of Effort and Ability of Local Districts to Support Public Schools," *Texas Outlook,* March 1941, 30.

58. Eby, 218.

59. Grantham, "Contours," 1047; Heck, "Educational Uplift," 5029; Cecil E. Evans, quoted in Tom W. Nichols, *Rugged Summit* (San Marcos: Southwest Texas State University Press, 1970), 469.

## CHAPTER 3

1. Vernon McDaniel, *History of the Teachers State Association of Texas* (Washington, D.C.: National Education Association, 1977), 28; Barr, *Black Texans,* 156; Richard Kluger, *Simple Justice: The History of* Brown v. Board of Education *and Black American's Struggle for Equality* (New York: Alfred A. Knopf, 1987), 115.

2. Joseph J. Rhoads, "Negro Educator Wants Prairie View College Developed as Modern A. & M. for his Race," *Dallas Morning News,* July 15, 1945.

3. Robert A. Margo, *Race and Schooling in the South, 1880–1950* (Chicago: University of Chicago Press, 1990), 6–8, 45.

4. Jo Ann Pankratz Stiles, "The Changing Economic and Educational Status of Texas Negroes, 1940–1960" (Master's thesis, University of Texas, 1966), 104; Dorothy Redus Robinson, *The Bell Rings at Four: A Black Teacher's Chronicle of Change* (Austin, Tex.: Madrona, 1978), 11, 4–5, 15; Senator James Taylor to Corrinne E. Crow, March 17, 1976, Aikin Oral History Project, 21.

5. Thad Sitton and Milam C. Rowold, *Ringing the Children In: Texas Country Schools* (College Station: Texas A&M University Press, 1987), 9; Barr, 99.

6. State Department of Education, *Negro Education in Texas,* Bulletin no. 294, September 1931 (Austin, Tex.: State Department of Education, 1931),

7. Clegg, 61; Sitton and Rowold, 50.

8. Guadalupe San Miguel Jr., and Richard R Valencia, "From the Treaty of Guadalupe Hidalgo to Hopwood: The Educational Plight and Struggle of Mexican Americans in the Southwest," *Harvard Educational Review* 68 (Fall 1998): 357; San Miguel, *"Let All of Them Take Heed,"* 10–14.

9. Arnoldo De León, *They Called Them Greasers: Anglo Attitudes Toward Mexicans in Texas, 1821–1900* (Austin: University of Texas Press, 1983), 105–6; Amilcar Shabazz, *Advancing Democracy: African Americans and the Struggle for Access and Equity in Higher Education in Texas* (Chapel Hill: University of North Carolina Press, 2004), 5; Neil Foley, *The White Scourge: Mexicans, Blacks, and Poor Whites in Texas Cotton Culture* (Berkeley: University of California Press, 1997), 41, 62; Blanton, *Strange Career of Bilingual Education,* 59–73.

10. Donald Johnson, "W. E. B. DuBois, Thomas Jesse Jones and the Struggle for Social Education, 1900–1930," *The Journal of Negro History* 85 (Summer 2000): 72.

11. William Edward Garnett, "Immediate and Pressing Race Problems of Texas," in *Proceedings of the Sixth Annual Convention of the Southwestern Political and Social Science Association Dallas Texas March 30–April 1, 1925,* edited by Caleb Perry Patterson (Austin, Tex.: Southwestern Political and Social Science Association, 1925), 36, 39–40.

12. See the three-part series by E. E. Davis, "Cotton and Farm Tenancy in West Texas," *Texas Outlook,* May 1925, 12–14, "King Cotton Leads Mexicans into Texas," *Texas Outlook,* April 1925, 7–9, and "Some Counties Annually Pay Less Than They Receive From the State Treasury," *Texas Outlook,* July 1925, 9–10. See Charles M. Wollenberg, *All Deliberate Speed: Segregation and Exclusion in California Schools, 1855–1975* (Berkeley: University of California Press, 1978).

13. Some have estimated the actual immigration was well over a million. See Carey

McWilliams, *North from Mexico: The Spanish-Speaking People of the United States* (Philadelphia: J. B. Lippincott, 1948), 163–64; San Miguel, *"Let All of Them Take Heed,"* 14–17.

14. McWilliams, *North from Mexico,* 163; Ernestine Alvarado, "Mexican Immigration to the United States," *Proceedings of the National Conference of Social Work in Chicago, 1920,* 479–80, in *Education in the United States,* vol. 15, ed. Sol Cohen (New York: Random House, 1974), 2929–30; John C. Box, "Peons from Mexico," *Texas Outlook,* July 1927, 32–33; Evan Anders, *Boss Rule in South Texas: The Progressive Era* (Austin: University of Texas Press, 1982), 141.

15. Davis, "King Cotton," 7–8.

16. Ibid., 8.

17. Ibid., 8–9; Ravitch, *Left Back,* 377.

18. Garnett, 40; E. A. Wood, "Digest of Texas Housing Laws," *Texas Municipalities,* February 1938, 31

19. Davis, "Some Counties," 9–10.

20. Isabel Fuentez Preuss, interviewed by author, June 23, 1990, New Braunfels, Texas, cassette and transcript, Southwest Texas State University, 2.

21. Albert Morales, "Reflections," interview by C. Herb Skoog (KGNB-AM, 25 August 1983), no. 330, Dittlinger Memorial Library, New Braunfels, Texas.

22. Annie Reynolds, *The Education of Spanish-Speaking Children in Five Southwestern States,* U. S. Department of the Interior, Office of Education, Bulletin 1933, No. 11 (Washington D.C.: United States Government Printing Office, 1933), 11.

23. Morales interview; McWilliams, *North from Mexico,* 298–99; George A. Works, "Summary of the Texas School Survey Report," *Texas Outlook,* August 1925, 25.

24. Reynolds, 11.

25. Walt W. Rostow, *The Diffusion of Power: An Essay in Recent History* (New York: Macmillan, 1972), 423.

26. Julie Leininger Pycior, *LBJ & Mexican Americans: The Paradox of Power* (Austin: University of Texas Press, 1997), 3–22; *Public Papers of the Presidents: Lyndon B. Johnson; Containing the Public Messages, Speeches, and Statements of the President, 1968* (Washington, D.C.: USGPO, 1965–1970), 1138.

27. Eunice Elvira Parr, "A Comparative Study of Mexican and American Children in the Schools of San Antonio, Texas" (Master's thesis, University of Chicago, 1926; reprint, San Francisco: R and E Research Associates, 1971), 44–45; Garnett, "Immediate and Pressing Race Problems," 31–35.

28. William O. Sisk, "The Mexicans in Texas Schools," *Texas Outlook,* December 1930, 10; Gilbert G. Gonzalez, *Chicano Education in the Era of Segregation* (Philadelphia: The Balch Institute Press, 1990), 62; San Miguel, *"Let All of Them Take Heed,"* 18–19.

29. *Gong Lum v. Rice,* 275 U.S. 78 (1927).

30. San Miguel, *"Let All of Them Take Heed,"* 78–80.

31. Thurgood Marshall, "An Evaluation of Recent Efforts to Achieve Racial Integration in Education Through Resort to the Courts," *Journal of Negro Education* 21 (Summer 1952): 317–18.

32. Margo, 53–55; Michael Fultz, "African American Teachers in the South, 1890–1940: Powerlessness and the Ironies of Expectations and Protest," *History of Education Quarterly* 35 (Winter 1995): 402; Bruce Beezer, "Black Teachers' Salaries and the Federal Courts Before *Brown v. Board of Education:* One Beginning for Equity," *Journal of Negro Education* 55 (Spring 1986): 201; Robinson, 39.

33. Beezer, "Black Teachers' Salaries," 201; National Association for the Advancement of Colored People, *Teachers' Salaries in Black and White: A Pamphlet for Teachers and Their Friends* (New York: NAACP, 1942), 4–5; Lawrence A. Cremin, *American Education: The Metropolitan Experience, 1876–1980* (New York: Harper and Row, 1988), 199; Kluger, 215–16.

34. Kate S. Kirkland, "For All Houston's Children: Ima Hogg and the Board of Education, 1943–1949," *Southwestern Historical Quarterly* 101 (April 1998): 476–78.

35. Irving G. Lang, letter to the editor, *Dallas Morning News,* December 16, 1940.

36. Richard M. Dalfiume, "The 'Forgotten Years' of the Negro Revolution," *Journal of American History* 55 (June 1968): 91–92.

37. Ibid., 98.

38. Dennis N. Valdes, "Legal Status and the Struggles of Farmworkers in West Texas and New Mexico, 1942–1993," *Latin American Perspectives* 22 (Winter 1995): 118–19.

39. Pauline R. Kibbe, *Latin Americans in Texas* (Albuquerque: University of New Mexico Press, 1946); *Dallas Morning News,* "Texas May Get Farm Workers from Mexico," March 7, 1949.

40. *Austin American,* June 16, 1948; Final Judgment, *Delgado v. Bastrop Independent School District,* No. 388, Civil District Court, Western District of Texas, June 15, 1948, in John J. Herrera Papers, Box 2, Folder 19, Houston Metropolitan Research Center, Houston Public Library, Houston, Texas.

41. Theodore Gilmore Bilbo, *Take Your Choice: Separation or Mongrelization* (Poplarville, Miss.: Dream House, 1947), 149.

42. United States, President's Committee on Civil Rights, *"To Secure These Rights": The Report of the President's Committee on Civil Rights* (New York: Simon & Schuster, 1947), 100–101.

43. Executive Order 9981, July 26, 1948, General Records of the United States Government, RG 11, National Archives, http://www.ourdocuments.gov/doc.php?flash=true&doc=84; For a critical analysis of the results of Executive Order 9981, see Otis M. Darden, "The Integration of Afro-Americans into the Army Mainstream, 1948–1954," (Master's thesis, U.S. Army Command and General Staff College, 1993).

44. Collier Anderson to Roosevelt, August 16, 1940, quoted in Richard Polenberg, *War and Society: The United States, 1941–1945* (New York: J. B. Lippincott, 1972), 99.

45. Patrick J. Carroll, *Felix Longoria's Wake: Bereavement, Racism, and the Rise of Mexican American Activism* (Austin: University of Texas Press, 2003), 66; Barr, *Black Texans,* 214–15.

46. "Lynch Law for Texas," *Dallas Morning News,* March 3, 1949; "Bill Prohibiting Mob Violence and Lynching Passed by House," *Dallas Morning News,* March 8, 1949; Beauford H. Jester, "Message from the Governor," February 16, 1949, House Journal, 51st Leg., R.S., 268–69.

47. *Dallas Morning News,* March 9, 1949.

48. *School: The Story of American Education,* Episode 2, *As American As School, 1900–1950,* Stone Lantern Films, New York, 2001.

49. Jorge Iber, "Mexican Americans of South Texas Football: The Athletic and Coaching Careers of E. C. Lerma and Bobby Cavazos, 1932–1965," *Southwestern Historical Quarterly* 105 (April 2002): 625–28.

50. Ibid., 630–32; Lauro F. Cavazos, *A Kineño Remembers: From the King Ranch to the White House* (College Station: Texas A&M University Press, 2006), 77–79, 83–84, 112–14.

51. *Brown v. Board Of Education,* 347 U.S. 483 (1954).

## CHAPTER 4

1. B. F. Vance, "The Food-for-Freedom Program," *Texas Outlook,* February 1942, 38.

2. "Texas Births Gain From 1940 to 1947," *Dallas Morning News,* March 7, 1949.

3. Seth S. McKay and Odie B. Faulk, *Texas After Spindletop,* The Saga of Texas Series, 1901–1965, ed. Seymour V. Connor (Austin, Tex.: Steck-Vaughn Company, 1965), 217; Green, 142; "Texas

Rolls Into Tideland Fight," *Austin American,* May 5, 1949; Richard M. Morehead, "The Tide-lands Stake—III: Schools of Texas Would Take Loss," *Dallas Morning News,* December 1, 1948.

4. McKay and Faulk, *Texas After Spindletop,* 191.

5. National Commission on School District Reorganization, *Your School District* (Washington, D.C.: Department of Rural Education, National Education Association, 1948), 37.

6. Ibid., 25–26.

7. Ibid., 27–28.

8. Ibid., 28–29.

9. Polenberg, *War and Society,* 3.

10. U.S. Department of Health, Education, and Welfare, Office of Education, *The State and Education: The Structure and Control of Public Education at the State Level,* by Fred F. Beach and Robert F. Will in cooperation with the Study Commission of the Council of Chief State School Officers, misc. no. 23 (Washington, D.C.: USGPO, 1955), 1–3.

11. Ronald D. Cohen, "Schooling Uncle Sam's Children: Education in the USA, 1941–1945," in *Education and the Second World War: Studies in Schooling and Social Change,* ed. Roy Lowe (London: The Falmer Press, 1992), 46–47.

12. James Bryant Conant, "Education for a Classless Society: The Jeffersonian Tradition," *Atlantic Monthly,* May 1940, http://www.theatlantic.com/issues/95sep/ets/edcla.htm (accessed on March 29, 2003).

13. James Bryant Conant, "Mobilizing American Youth," *Atlantic Monthly,* July 1942, http://www.theatlantic.com/issues/95sep/ets/moam.htm (accessed on March 30, 2003).

14. J. Manley Head to Corrinne E. Crow, May 28, 1975, Aikin Oral History Project, 26.

15. "A Report from the Baltimore Meetings," *Education for Victory,* 20 December 1944, 4.

16. Ibid., 5.

17. Ibid.

18. Ibid., 11–12.

19. Alexander J. Stoddard, "Shall We Pinch Pennies for Peace?" *Education for Victory,* January 3, 1945, 1.

20. John A. McCarthy, "Preparation for More Effective Living," *Education for Victory,* January 3, 1945, 4.

21. Francis T. Spaulding, "What Kind of High School Do You Want?" *Ladies Home Journal,* August 1948, 48, 166–67.

22. U.S. Department of Health, Education, and Welfare, Office of Education, *Public School Finance Programs of the United States,* by Clayton D. Hutchins and Albert R. Munse, misc. no. 22 (Washington, D.C.: USGPO, 1955), 1.

23. Dean Larry Haskew to Corrinne E. Crow, August 7, 1978, Aikin Oral History Project, 17.

24. Lowry Nelson, "The American Rural Heritage," *American Quarterly* 1 (Fall 1949): 230.

25. Edgar L. Morphet, *Improving Education in the Southern States,* Committee on State and Local Financing of Public Schools Bulletin no. 1, 1941 (Tallassee, Ala.: Southern States Work-Conference on School Administrative Problems, 1941), 23–24.

26. Albert S. Goss, "Educated, Skilled Farm Population," *Education for Victory,* 3 January 1945, 5.

27. National Commission, *Your School District,* 34.

28. George Q. Flynn, *The Draft, 1940–1973* (Lawrence: University of Kansas Press, 1993), 31–32; Vance, "Food-for-Freedom Program," 38.

29. National Commission, *Your School District,* 34; Dosca Hale, "Build for Defense With Good Food Habits," *Texas Outlook,* October 1941, 35; Vance, "The Food-for-Freedom Program," 38.

30. U.S. Federal Security Agency, Office of Education, *Curriculum Adjustments for the Mentally Retarded: A Guide for Elementary and Secondary Schools,* ed. Elise H. Martens, Bulletin 1950, No. 2, 2nd ed. (Washington, D.C.: USGPO 1950), 7; E. J. Cummins, M.D., "Improving Health and Physical Education in the Texas Schools," *Texas Outlook,* November 1942, 10.

31. D. K. Brace, "H.R. 1074: National Preparedness Act for the Improvement of Physical and Social Fitness," *Texas Outlook,* April 1941, 13.

32. "Texas Among 'First 12' States in Illiteracy Draft Rejections," *Dallas Morning News,* April 2, 1948.

33. John K. Norton, "The Myth of Educational Equality," *American Mercury,* January 1946, 16–17.

34. "Resolutions Passed by House of Delegates," *Texas Outlook,* January 1946, 22.

35. Irene Dunne, "Teachers Underpaid," *Texas Outlook,* January 1946, 42; Robert Littell, "Teachers' Pay—A National Disgrace," *Texas Outlook,* January 1946, 15.

36. Littell, 15.

37. H. K. Moore, "Physicians, Don't let them Socialize you," *Texas Outlook,* January 1946, 48.

38. Ibid.

39. B. B. Cobb, "As We See It, 'Teacher Shortage,'" *Texas Outlook,* February 1946, 6.

40. Kirkland, 485.

41. "Looking at the Forty-Eight State School Systems," *Texas Outlook,* October 1949, 17. The results showed 963 had less than two years of college; 8,293 had between two and four years of college; 29,636 had their bachelor's degree and 5,607 had master's degrees in the 1947–48 school year.

42. "Textbooks," *Time,* November 1, 1937, http://www.time.com/time/magazine/article/0,9171,882911,00.html (accessed on June 7, 2008).

43. Letter from J. B. Bright to A. M. Aikin, May 17, 1947, Box 5, Folder 5-7, General Correspondence, 1945–47, A. M. Aikin Jr. Papers, 1937–1959.

44. Frank W. Richardson, "Wanted!: A Financial Wizard for our Equalization Aid Schools," *Texas Outlook,* February 1948, 15.

45. Floyd H. Burton, "Scholastic Census as a Basis for Distributing School Funds," *Texas Outlook,* December 1948, 15.

46. Senator James Taylor to Corrinne E. Crow, March 17, 1976, Aikin Oral History Project, 23.

47. Ibid.; Burton, 15.

48. Preston Smith to David Murrah, June 28, 1990, Oral History Collection, Southwest Collection/Special Collection Library, Texas Tech University Libraries, Lubbock, Texas.

49. Edgar L. Morphet, "What Should Teachers Know About School Finance?" *Texas Outlook,* June 1949, 19.

50. Dean Larry Haskew to Corrinne E. Crow, August 7, 1978, Aikin Oral History Project, 19.

## CHAPTER 5

1. Speaker Claud Gilmer to Corrinne E. Crow, November 14, 1976, Aikin Oral History Project, 19–20.

2. Ibid., 20–21.

3. Elizabeth Koch, "Greetings," *Texas Outlook,* January 1946, 11.

4. Sarah Gaskill, "Concerning Salary Schedules," *Texas Outlook,* February 1946, 40.

5. Still, 11–15.

6. Ibid.

7. Senator James Taylor to Corrinne E. Crow, March 17, 1976, Aikin Oral History Project, 20.

8. House Concurrent Resolution 48, House Journal, 50th Leg., R.S., 700.

9. Still, 17.

10. Ibid., 17–20.

11. Frances T. Davis, "The Role of Senator A. M. Aikin, Jr., in the Development of Public Education in Texas, 1932–1974" (ED diss., East Texas State University, 1975), 52.

12. Welma Aikin to Corrinne E. Crow, July 10 and 11, 1974, Aikin Oral History Project, 19.

13. Ibid., 25; Davis, 56.

14. Davis, 57.

15. "Noted Texas Senator A. M. Aikin Jr. Dies," *Lubbock Avalanche-Journal,* October 26, 1981.

16. James Taylor interview, 51–52; Senator William Moore to Corrinne E. Crow, February 27, 1975, Aikin Oral History Project, 20.

17. Sam Kinch Jr., "A. M. Aikin, One of the State's 'Most Revered Leaders,' Dies," *Dallas Morning News,* October 26, 1981; "Noted Texas Senator A. M. Aikin Jr. Dies;" Colonel Dean Aikin to Corrinne E. Crow, August 1, 1974, Aikin Oral History Project, 23–24.

18. Welma Aikin interview, 44.

19. C. H. Gilmer obituary, *Austin American Statesman,* February 27, 1983; Vicki J. Audette and J. Tom Graham, *Claud H. Gilmer: Lone Star Lawmaker and Country Lawyer* (Rocksprings, Tex.: Carson Gilmer and Norma Jean Babb, 2003), 23–43, 120–22.

20. Still, 20–21.

21. Ibid., 21.

22. James Taylor interview, 26; 1991, University of California: In Memoriam, "Edgar L. Morphet, Education: Berkeley," http://dynaweb.oac.cdlib.org:8088/dynaweb/uchist/public/inmemoriam/inmemoriam1991/@Generic__BookTextView/2439;pt=239 (accessed on November 12, 2003); Memo from James E. Taylor, November 6, 1947 to All Co-Chairmen, Gilmer-Aikin Committee, "Correspondence October 11, 1947 to March 2, 1949 and Undated," Box 3H110, Gilmer-Aiken [*sic*] Records, 1947–1949, The Center for American History, University of Texas at Austin (hereafter cited as Gilmer-Aiken Records).

23. Claud Gilmer to Corrinne E. Crow, November 15, 1976, Aikin Oral History Project, 4; Still, 24–25.

24. Still, 25–26.

25. Ibid.; Letter from H. A. Moore to County Advisory Committees, April 27, 1948, "Correspondence October 11, 1947 to March 2, 1949 and Undated," Box 3H110, Gilmer-Aiken Records.

26. Texas Legislature, Gilmer-Aikin Committee on Education, *To Have What We Must . . . : A Digest of Proposals to Improve Public Education in Texas* (Austin, 1948), 13–39.

27. Audette and Graham, 139; Still, 32.

28. Still, 31–35.

29. Ibid., 20; James Taylor interview, 24.

30. Still, 37.

31. Ibid., 38–40.

32. Ibid., 57; Sam Kinch and Stuart Long, *Allan Shivers: The Pied Piper of Texas Politics* (Austin, Tex.: Shoal Creek Publishers, 1973), 46–47.

33. Senator William Moore to Corrinne E. Crow, February 27, 1975, Aikin Oral History Project, 2.

34. Senator James Taylor to Corrinne E. Crow, March 17, 1976, Aikin Oral History Project, 21.

35. Mrs. Martin A. Row, letter to Senator James E. Taylor, February 24, 1949, attached to handwritten note marked, "Given," League of Women Voters of Texas Records, 1920–1971, State Files, 1922–1970, Program Files, 1923–1970, Folder 7 Education, Gilmen [sic]–Aikin Bill, 1947–1951, Southwest Collection/Special Collections Library, Texas Tech University Libraries, Lubbock, Texas.

36. W. C. McGehee to Beauford Jester, December 29, 1948, Records of Beauford H. Jester, Texas Office of the Governor, Archives and Information Services Division, Texas State Library and Archives Commission (hereafter cited as Records of Beauford H. Jester); Still, *Gilmer-Aikin Bills,* 32–33; Mrs. Leroy Roberts to Beauford Jester, 6 January 1949, Records of Beauford H. Jester.

37. Stephen C. Anderson, *J. W. Edgar: Educator for Texas* (Austin, Tex.: Eakin, 1984), 77; Horace Carl Elliott, "L. A. Woods: State Superintendent of Public Instruction in Texas" (Master's thesis, Hardin Simmons University, 1947), 22–25.

38. L. A. Woods, "Texas and the Other 47 States," *Texas Outlook,* October 1949, 24–25.

39. Ibid.

40. Ibid., 103.

41. W. V. Harrison, "Appoint All Officials," Letters from Readers, *Dallas Morning News,* March 7, 1949.

42. Jay Vessels, "Foes May Seek Court Test of Key G-A Bill," *Austin American,* May 5, 1949, 1; Letter from A. M. Aikin to Ben Peek, January 18, 1949, Box 9, Folder 9-4, General Correspondence, 1945–1947, A. M. Aikin Jr. Papers; Letter from A. M. Aikin to E. A. Millsap, April 11, 1947, Box 7, Folder 7-2, General Correspondence, 1945–47, A. M. Aikin Jr. Papers.

43. Green, 118; Letter from Adolph Till to O. E. Cannon, March 2, 1949, "Correspondence October 11, 1947 to March 2, 1949 and Undated," Box 3H110, Gilmer-Aiken Records; San Miguel, *"Let All of Them Take Heed,"* 128–29.

44. Speaker Claud Gilmer to Corrinne E. Crow, November 15, 1976, Aikin Oral History Project, 38–39.

45. L. P. Sturgeon, oral history interview by Corrinne Crow, transcript, 16 January 1976, Aikin Oral History Project, 7; L. A. Woods to A. M. Aikin Jr., 27 January 1949, to A. M. Aikin, A. M. Aikin Jr. Papers, 1937–1959, Subject Correspondence, 51st Leg., 1949, Box 23, Gilmer-Aikin Committee, Folder 13, University Archives, James G. Gee Library, Texas A&M University–Commerce (hereafter cited A. M. Aikin Jr., Papers).

46. Anderson, *J. W. Edgar,* 84–85; Alonzo Wasson, "Gilmer-Aikin Advocates Have Effective Argument," *Dallas Morning News,* March 4, 1949.

47. Virginia Forbes, "School Ruling Helps Restore Latin Relations," *Austin American,* June 16, 1948; "Texas Eliminates False Prejudice," *Dallas Morning News,* June 18, 1948; Jorge C. Rangel and Carlos M. Alcala, "Project Report: De Jure Segregation of Chicanos in Texas Schools," *Harvard Civil Rights–Civil Liberties Law Review* 7 (March 1972): 339.

48. Anderson, *J. W. Edgar,* 95.

49. Still, 87–88.

50. Ibid., 91–97.

51. Ibid., 98–121.

52. Ibid., 122–25.

53. Ibid., 125–140.

54. Ibid., 141–43, 152–54,

## CHAPTER 6

1. Irwin Wilson, letter to A. M. Aikin, January 15, 1947, Folder 23-14, Box 23, Subject Correspondence, 1947, 1949 Per Capita Bills—Gladewater Plan, A. M. Aikin Jr., Papers, 1939–1945.

2. Raymond Brooks, "Lobbying Changes from Professional to Amateur Status," *Austin American,* May 4, 1949; Still, 84.

3. Alonzo Wasson, "School Committee Hedges on One Vital Proposal," *Dallas Morning News,* December 8, 1948.

4. Speaker Claud Gilmer to Corrinne E. Crow, November 15, 1976, Aikin Oral History Project, 19-22; *Houston Post,* October 28, 1981.

5. Howard C. Doolittle (Principal Emerson Junior School; San Antonio Independent School District) to A. M. Aikin, May 17, 1949, Folder 23-14, Box 23, Subject Correspondence, 1947, 1949 Per Capita Bills—Gladewater Plan, A. M. Aikin Jr. Papers, 1939–1945.

6. Stella Mae Crain (corresponding secretary Paris Classroom Teachers Association) to A. M. Aikin, March 18, 1949, Folder 23-14, Box 23, Subject Correspondence, 1947, 1949 Per Capita Bills—Gladewater Plan, A. M. Aikin Jr. Papers, 1939–1945.

7. Mrs. W. B. Burkhalter (Amarillo Public Schools) to A. M. Aikin, May 13, 1949, Folder 23-14, Box 23, Subject Correspondence, 1947, 1949 Per Capita Bills—Gladewater Plan, A. M. Aikin Jr. Papers, 1939–1945.

8. Emma Mae Brotze, (Principal, Marshall Junior-Senior High School) to A. M. Aikin, May 5, 1949, Folder 23-14, Box 23, Subject Correspondence, 1947,1949 Per Capita Bills—Gladewater Plan, A. M. Aikin Jr. Papers, 1939–1945.

9. C. O. Chandler (Superintendent, Orange Public Schools) to A. M. Aikin, May 18, 1949, Folder 23-14, Box 23, Subject Correspondence, 1947, 1949 Per Capita Bills—Gladewater Plan, A. M. Aikin Jr. Papers, 1939–1945.

10. Letter from Frank C. Bean to A. M. Aikin, June 4, 1947, Box 5, Folder 5-7, General Correspondence, 1945–47, A. M. Aikin Jr. Papers, 1937–1959.

11. University of Texas, *Rural School Education: Lectures Delivered and Outlines of Round Tables Held During Rural School Education Week Under the Auspices of the University Summer Schools, July 15–19, 1912,* Bulletin 251 (Austin: University of Texas, 1912), 83.

12. Undated, handwritten notecard, Box 38, Folder 38-18 Gilmer-Aikin Committee—Reports and Pamphlets, 51st Leg., 1949, A. M. Aikin Jr. Papers, 1937–1959.

13. Audette and Graham, 289.

14. Joe C. Humphrey, "Texas' New School Laws," *Texas Outlook,* July 1949, 14; Mrs. Ruth Carter (principal P. F. Brown School, Lubbock Public Schools) to A. M. Aikin, May 31, 1949, Folder 23-14, Box 23, Subject Correspondence, 1947, 1949 Per Capita Bills—Gladewater Plan, A. M. Aikin Jr. Papers, 1939–1945.

15. William R. Powell to Gene B. Preuss, July 7, 1995, Oral History Collection, Southwest Collection/Special Collections Library, Texas Tech University, Lubbock, Texas.

16. Imogene Jinkins, "To Gilmer-Aikin Salaries—Nuts!" *Texas Outlook,* February 1950, 25.

17. Kenneth H. Kidwell, "Effects of G-A Legislation on Teacher Shortage," *Texas Outlook,* July 1950, 18.

18. James E. Taylor, "Gilmer-Aikin Program and State Finances," *East Texas,* January 1950, 13; J. Warren Hitt, "Trends in Texas Schools," *Texas Observer,* April 1950, 24; Texas Commission on Higher Education, *Report to The Honorable Allan Shivers, Governor of Texas and The Legislature of the State of Texas,* November 4, 1954 (Austin: Texas Education Association, 1954), 1.

19. William E. Moreland, "Houston's Public School System, 1949–1950," William E. Moreland Collection, Mss 6, Box 6F1, Houston Metropolitan Research Collection, Houston Public Library, Houston, Texas; E. L. Wildman, "Kerrville Kids are Healthier—thanks to G-A legislation," *Texas Outlook,* June 1950, 10.

20. David Tyack, Robert Lowe, and Elizabeth Hansot, *Public Schools in Hard Times: The Great Depression and Recent Years* (Cambridge, Mass.: Harvard University Press, 1984), 28; Luther Pearson, "Gilmer-Aikin Proposals," *Texas Outlook,* January 1949, 4.

21. Burton R. Clark, ed, *The Problems of American Education* (New York: New York Times Company, 1975), 11.

22. "Duties and Responsibilities of the Commissioner of Education," *Texas Outlook,* October 1950, 17; "G-A Results," *Texas Outlook,* September 1950, 17.

23. *McKinney v. Blankenship,* 282 S.W.2d 691, 697 (Tex. 1955).

24. Fred C. Ayer and J. C. Conradt, "They Learn By Doing," *Texas Outlook,* April 1950, 17.

25. Lizabeth Cohen, *A Consumer's Republic: The Politics of Mass Consumption in Postwar America* (New York: Alfred A. Knopf, 2003), 244.

26. James E. Taylor, "Gilmer-Aikin Program and State Finances," *East Texas,* January 1950, 12.

27. J. Warren Hitt, "Trends in Texas Schools," *Texas Observer,* April 1950, 24.

28. Joseph R. Griggs, "Better Schools Cost Less," *Texas Outlook,* March 1950, 12.

29. Morphet, "What Should Teachers Know?" 19.

30. Ibid., 18–19, 39.

31. Ibid.; Pearson, 4.

32. A. M. Aikin's name honors an elementary school in Paris, Texas; Dallas; and the New Caney ISO. The University of Texas has two A. M. Aikin Regents Chairs: one in Education Leadership, and the other in Community College Leadership.

33. A. M. Aikin vertical file, Center for American History, the University of Texas at Austin.

# BIBLIOGRAPHY

## ARCHIVAL MATERIAL

Aikin, A. M., Jr. Papers. University Archives. James G. Gee Library. Texas A&M University-Commerce.

"Aikin, A. M." Vertical File. Center for American History. The University of Texas at Austin.

Gilmer-Aiken [*sic*] Records. 1947–1949. The Center for American History. University of Texas at Austin.

Hawkins, Walace. Literary Effort. Archive and Information Services Division. Texas State Library and Archive Commission. Austin, Texas.

Herrera, John J. Papers. Houston Metropolitan Research Center. Houston Public Library. Houston, Texas.

Jester, Beauford H. Papers. Texas Office of the Governor. Archives and Information Services Division, Texas State Library and Archives Commission (hereafter cited as ARIS—TSLAC).

League of Women Voters of Texas. Records. Southwest Collection/Special Collection Library. Texas Tech University Libraries.

Moreland, William E. Collection. Houston Metropolitan Research Collection. Houston (Texas) Public Library.

O'Daniel, W. Lee. Papers. Texas Office of the Governor. ARIS—TSLAC.

University of California History Digital Archives. "Edgar L. Morphet, Education: Berkeley." *University of California: In Memoriam, 1991.* http://dynaweb.oac.cdlib.org:8088/dynaweb/uchist/public/@Generic__CollectionView (accessed on November 12, 2003).

## ARTICLES AND CHAPTERS

Anderson, James D. "Race, Meritocracy, and the American Academy during the Immediate Post-World War II Era." *History of Education Quarterly* 33 (Summer 1993): 150–175.

Baker, Scott. "Testing Equality: The National Teacher Examination and the NAACP's Legal Campaign to Equalize Teachers' Salaries in the South, 1936–63." *History of Education Quarterly* 35 (Spring 1995): 49–64.

Beezer, Bruce. "Black Teachers' Salaries and the Federal Courts Before Brown v. Board of Education: One Beginning for Equity." *Journal of Negro Education* 55 (Spring 1986): 200–214.

Berger, Max. "Stephen F. Austin and Education in Early Texas, 1821–1835." *Southwestern Historical Quarterly* 48 (January 1948): 387–394.

Bracey, Gerald W. "What Happened to America's Public Schools?" *American Heritage,* November 1997.

Cohen, Ronald D. "Schooling Uncle Sam's Children: Education in the USA, 1941–1945." In

*Education and the Second World War: Studies in Schooling and Social Change,* edited by Roy Lowe, 46–58. London: The Falmer Press, 1992.

Crouch, Barry A. "A Spirit of Lawlessness: White Violence; Texas Blacks, 1865–1868." *Journal of Social History* 18 (Winter 1984): 217–232.

Dalfiume, Richard M. "The 'Forgotten Years' of the Negro Revolution." *Journal of American History* 55 (June 1968): 90–106.

Elliott, Claude. "The Freedmen's Bureau in Texas." *Southwestern Historical Quarterly* 56 (July 1952): 1–24.

Finkle, Lee. "The Conservative Aims of Militant Rhetoric: Black Protest during World War II." *Journal of American History* 60 (December 1973): 692–713.

Friend, Llerena B. "The Texan of 1860." *Southwestern Historical Quarterly* 62 (July 1958): 1–17.

Fultz, Michael. "African American Teachers in the South, 1890–1940: Powerlessness and the Ironies of Expectations and Protest." *History of Education Quarterly* 35 (Winter 1995): 401–422.

———. "Teacher Training and African American Education in the South, 1900–1940." *Journal of Negro Education* 64 (Spring 1995): 196–210.

Garnett, William Edward. "Immediate and Pressing Race Problems of Texas." In *Proceedings of the Sixth Annual Convention of the Southwestern Political and Social Science Association Dallas Texas March 30–April 1, 1925,* edited by Caleb Perry Patterson. Austin: Southwestern Political and Social Science Association, 1925.

Grantham, Dewey W., Jr. "Texas Congressional Leaders and the New Freedom, 1913–1917." *Southwestern Historical Quarterly,* 53 (July 1949): 35–48.

———. "The Contours of Southern Progressivism." *American Historical Review* 86 (1981): 1035–59.

Hatcher, Mattie Austin. "Plan of Stephen F. Austin for an Institute of Modern Languages at San Felipe de Austin." *Texas Historical Association Quarterly* 12 (January 1909): 231–39.

Hornsby, Alton, Jr. "The Freedmen's Bureau Schools in Texas, 1865–1870." *Southwestern Historical Quarterly* 76 (April 1973): 397–417.

Iber, Jorge. "Mexican Americans of South Texas Football: The Athletic and Coaching Careers of E. C. Lerma and Bobby Cavazos, 1932–1965." *Southwestern Historical Quarterly* 105 (April 2002): 617–633.

Johnson, Donald. "W. E. B. DuBois, Thomas Jesse Jones and the Struggle for Social Education, 1900–1930." *The Journal of Negro History* 85 (Summer 2000): 71–95.

Kirkland, Kate S. "For All Houston's Children: Ima Hogg and the Board of Education, 1943–1949." *Southwestern Historical Quarterly* 101 (4): 460–495.

Koos, Leonard V. "The Fruits of School Surveys." *Schools and Society* 5 (January 13, 1917): 35–41.

Link, Arthur S. "The Wilson Movement in Texas, 1910–1912." *Southwestern Historical Quarterly* 48 (October 1944): 169–185.

———. "The Progressive Movement in the South, 1870–1914." *North Carolina Historical Review* 23 (April 1946): 172–195.

———. "What Happened to the Progressive Movement in the 1920's?" *American Historical Review* 64 (July 1959): 833–851.

Marshall, Thurgood. "An Evaluation of Recent Efforts to Achieve Racial Integration in Education Through Resort to the Courts." *Journal of Negro Education* 21 (Summer 1952): 316–327.

Mitchell, Broadus. "Growth of Manufactures in the South." *Annals of the American Academy* 153 (January 1931): 21–29.

Moneyhon, Carl H. "Public Education and Texas Reconstruction." *Southwestern Historical Quarterly* 92 (January 1989): 393–416.

Nelson, Lowry. "The American Rural Heritage." *American Quarterly* 1 (Fall 1949): 225–234.

Pessen, Edward. "How Different from Each Other Were the Antebellum North and South?" *American Historical Review* 85 (December 1980): 1119–1149.

San Miguel, Guadalupe, Jr., and Richard R Valencia. "From the Treaty of Guadalupe Hidalgo to Hopwood: The Educational Plight and Struggle of Mexican Americans in the Southwest." *Harvard Educational Review* 68 (Fall 1998): 353–412.

Sitkoff, Harvard. "Racial Militancy and Interracial Violence in the Second World War." *Journal of American History* 58 (December 1971): 661–681.

Spearman, Mindy. "'Everything to Help, Nothing to Hinder': The Story of the *Texas School Journal*." *Southwestern Historical Quarterly* 111 (January 2008): 283–302.

Taylor, James E. "Gilmer-Aikin Program and State Finances." *East Texas,* January 1950.

Taylor, William R. "Toward a Definition of Orthodoxy: The Patrician South and the Common Schools." *Harvard Education Review* 36 (Fall 1966): 412–426.

Thompson, Holland. "Some Effects of Industrialism in an Agricultural State." *South Atlantic Quarterly* 4 (January 1905): 71–77.

Tyack, David B. "The Tribe and the Common School: Community Control in Rural Education." *American Quarterly* 24 (March 1972): 3–19.

Valdes, Dennis N. "Legal Status and the Struggles of Farmworkers in West Texas and New Mexico, 1942–1993." *Latin American Perspectives* 22 (Winter 1995): 117–137.

Wood, E. A. "Digest of Texas Housing Laws," *Texas Municipalities,* February 1938, 31.

## BOOKS

Alvarado, Ernestine. "Mexican Immigration to the United States," *Proceedings of the National Conference of Social Work in Chicago, 1920,* 479–80, in *Education in the United States,* vol. 15, edited by Sol Cohen. New York: Random House, 1974, 2929–30;

Anders, Evan. *Boss Rule in South Texas: The Progressive Era.* Austin: University of Texas Press, 1982.

Anderson, James D. *The Education of Blacks in the South.* Chapel Hill: University of North Carolina Press, 1988.

Anderson, Stephen C. *J. W. Edgar: Educator for Texas.* Austin, Tex.: Eakin, 1984.

Audette, Vicki J., and J. Tom Graham. *Claud H. Gilmer: Lone Star Lawmaker and Country Lawyer.* Rocksprings, Tex.: Carson Gilmer and Norma Jean Babb, 2003.

Barr, Alwyn. *Black Texans: A History of African Americans in Texas, 1528–1995.* 2nd ed. Norman: University of Oklahoma Press, 1996.

———. *Reconstruction to Reform: Texas Politics, 1876–1906.* 1971. Reprint, Dallas: Southern Methodist University Press, 2000.

Bennett, Michael J. *When Dreams Came True: The GI Bill and the Making of Modern America.* Washington, D.C.: Brassey's, 1996.

Bilbo, Theodore Gilmore. *Take Your Choice: Separation or Mongrelization.* Poplarville, Miss.: Dream House, 1947.

Blanton, Carlos Kevin. *The Strange Career of Bilingual Education in Texas, 1836–1981.* College Station: Texas A&M University Press, 2004.

Callahan, Raymond E. *Education and the Cult of Efficiency: A Study of the Social Forces That*

*Have Shaped the Administration of the Public Schools.* Chicago: University of Chicago Press, 1962.

Calvert, Robert A., and Arnoldo de León. *The History of Texas.* 2nd ed. Wheeling, Ill.: Harlan Davidson, 1996.

Campbell, Randolph B. *An Empire for Slavery: The Peculiar Institution in Texas, 1821–1865.* Baton Rouge: Louisiana State University Press, 1989.

———. *Gone to Texas: A History of the Lone Star State.* New York: Oxford University Press, 2003.

Carroll, Patrick J. *Felix Longoria's Wake: Bereavement, Racism, and the Rise of Mexican American Activism.* Austin: University of Texas Press, 2003.

Caswell, Hollis Leland. *City School Surveys: An Interpretation and Appraisal.* New York: Teachers College, Columbia University, 1929.

Cavazos, Lauro F. *A Kineño Remembers: From the King Ranch to the White House.* College Station: Texas A&M University Press, 2006.

Clark, Burton R., ed. *The Problems of American Education.* New York: New York Times Company, 1975.

Clegg, Luther Bryan, ed. *The Empty Schoolhouse: Memories of One-Room Texas Schools.* College Station: Texas A&M University Press, 1997.

Cohen, Lizabeth. *A Consumer's Republic: The Politics of Mass Consumption in Postwar America.* New York: Alfred A. Knopf, 2003.

Cottrell, Debbie Mauldin. *Pioneer Woman Educator: The Progressive Spirit of Annie Webb Blanton.* College Station: Texas A&M University Press, 1993.

Cremin, Lawrence A. *The Transformation of the School: Progressivism in American Education, 1876–1957.* New York: Alfred A. Knopf, 1961.

———. *American Education: The Metropolitan Experience, 1876–1980.* New York: Harper and Row, 1988.

Crouch, Barry A. *The Freedmen's Bureau and Black Texans.* Austin: University of Texas Press, 1992.

Curry, J. L. M. *A Brief Sketch of George Peabody, and a History of the Peabody Education Fund Through Thirty Years.* 1898. Reprint, New York: Negro University Press, 1969.

Danbom, David B. *The World of Hope: Progressives and the Struggle for an Ethical Public Life.* Philadelphia: Temple University Press, 1987.

———. *Born in the Country: A History of Rural America.* Baltimore: Johns Hopkins University Press, 1995.

Davis, William R. *The Development and Present Status of Negro Education in East Texas.* New York: Teachers College, Columbia University, 1934.

De León, Arnoldo. *They Called Them Greasers: Anglo Attitudes Toward Mexicans in Texas, 1821–1900.* Austin: University of Texas Press, 1983.

Doyle, Don H. *New Men, New Cities, New South: Atlanta, Nashville, Charleston, Mobile, 1860–1910.* Chapel Hill: University of North Carolina Press, 1990.

Eaton, Clement. *Growth of Southern Civilization, 1790–1860.* New York: Harper, 1961.

Eby, Frederick. *The Development of Education in Texas.* New York: Macmillan, 1925.

Evans, C. E. *The Story of Texas Schools.* Austin, Tex.: The Steck Company, 1955.

Fairclough, Adam. *Teaching Equality: Black Schools in the Age of Jim Crow.* Athens, Ga.: University of Georgia Press, 2001.

Federal Security Agency. Office of Education. *Curriculum Adjustments for the Mentally Retarded: A Guide for Elementary and Secondary Schools.* 2nd ed. Revised by Elise H. Martens. Washington, D.C.: USGPO 1950.

Fine, Benjamin. *Our Children Are Cheated: The Crisis in American Education.* New York: Henry Holt, 1947.

Flynn, George Q. *The Draft, 1940–1973.* Lawrence: University of Kansas Press, 1993.

Foley, Neil. *The White Scourge: Mexicans, Blacks, and Poor Whites in Texas Cotton Culture.* Berkeley: University of California Press, 1997.

Gaston, Paul M. *The New South Creed: A Study in Southern Mythmaking.* New York: Knopf, 1970.

Gonzalez, Gilbert G. *Chicano Education in the Era of Segregation.* Philadelphia: The Balch Institute Press, 1990.

Gould, Lewis. *Progressives and Prohibitionists: Texas Democrats in the Wilson Era.* Austin: University of Texas Press, 1973.

Gould, Lewis, ed. *The Progressive Era.* Syracuse, N.Y.: Syracuse University Press, 1974.

Grantham, Dewey W. *Southern Progressivism: The Reconciliation of Progress and Tradition.* Knoxville: University of Tennessee Press, 1983.

Green, George Norris. *The Establishment in Texas Politics: The Primitive Years, 1938–1957.* Norman: University of Oklahoma Press, 1979.

Hofstadter, Richard. *The Age of Reform: From Bryan to F.D.R.* New York: Alfred A. Knopf, 1955.

Hofstadter, Richard, ed., *The Progressive Movement.* Englewood Cliffs, N.J.: Prentice Hall, 1963.

Hogan, William Ransom. *The Texas Republic: A Social and Economic History.* Austin: University of Texas Press, 1969.

Johnson, Lyndon B. *Public Papers of the Presidents: Lyndon B. Johnson, 1968.* Washington, D.C.: USGPO, 1965–1970.

Kaestle, Carl F. *Pillars of the Republic: Common Schools and American Society, 1780–1860.* New York: Hill and Wang, 1983.

Kibbe, Pauline R. *Latin Americans in Texas.* Albuquerque: University of New Mexico Press, 1946.

Kinch, Sam, and Stuart Long. *Allan Shivers: The Pied Piper of Texas Politics.* Austin, Tex.: Shoal Creek Publishers, 1973.

Kluger, Richard. *Simple Justice: The History of* Brown v. Board of Education *and Black American's Struggle for Equality.* New York: Alfred A. Knopf, 1987.

Leloudis, James L. *Schooling in the New South: Pedagogy, Self, and Society in North Carolina, 1880–1920.* Chapel Hill: University of North Carolina Press, 1996.

Link, William A. *A Hard Country and a Lonely Place: Schooling, Society, and Reform in Rural Virginia, 1870–1920.* Chapel Hill: University of North Carolina Press, 1986.

———. *The Paradox of Southern Progressivism, 1880–1930.* Chapel Hill: University of North Carolina Press, 1992.

Margo, Robert A. *Race and Schooling in the South, 1880–1950.* Chicago: University of Chicago Press, 1990.

McDaniel, Vernon. *History of the Teachers State Association of Texas.* Washington, D.C.: National Education Association, 1977.

McKay, Seth Shepard. *W. Lee O'Daniel and Texas Politics, 1938–1942.* Lubbock: Texas Tech Press, 1944.

McKay, Seth Shepard, and Odie B. Faulk. *Texas After Spindletop.* Austin: Steck-Vaughn Company, 1965.

McWilliams, Carey. *North from Mexico: The Spanish-Speaking People of the United States.* Philadelphia: J. B. Lippincott, 1948.

Montejano, David. *Anglos and Mexicans in the Making of Texas, 1836–1986*. Austin: University of Texas Press, 1987.

Morphet, Edgar L. *Improving Education in the Southern States*. Tallahassee, Fla.: Southern States Work-Conference on School Administrative Problems, 1941.

Mort, Paul R., and Walter C. Reusser. *Public School Finances: Its Background, Structure, and Operations*. New York: McGraw-Hill, 1941.

National Association for the Advancement of Colored People. *Teachers' Salaries in Black and White*. Legal Defense and Educational Fund, Inc. 1942.

National Education Association. Department of Rural Education. National Commission on School District Reorganization. *Your School District*. Washington, D.C.: National Education Association, 1948.

National Research Council. Committee on Education Finance. Commission on Behavioral and Social Sciences and Education. *Equity and Adequacy in Education Finance: Issues and Perspectives*. Edited by Helen F. Ladd, Rosemary Chalk, and Janet S. Hansen. Washington, D.C.: National Academy Press, 1999.

Nichols, Tom W. *Rugged Summit*. San Marcos: Southwest Texas State University Press, 1970.

Nunn, W. C. *Texas Under the Carpetbaggers*. Austin: University of Texas Press, 1962.

Owens, William A. *This Stubborn Soil: A Frontier Boyhood*. 1986. Reprint, New York: Scribner, 1966.

Parkerson, Donald H., and Jo Ann Parkerson. *Transitions in American Education: A Social History of Teaching*. New York: RoutledgeFalmer, 2001.

Peterson, Paul E. *The Politics of School Reform, 1870–1940*. Chicago: University of Chicago Press, 1985.

Polenberg, Richard. *War and Society: The United States, 1941–1945*. New York: J. B. Lippincott, 1972.

Pycior, Julie Leininger. *LBJ & Mexican Americans: The Paradox of Power*. Austin: University of Texas Press, 1997.

Ravitch, Diane. *Left Back: A Century of Battles Over School Reform*. New York: Simon & Schuster, 2000.

Robinson, Dorothy Redus. *The Bell Rings at Four: A Black Teacher's Chronicle of Change*. Austin, Tex.: Madrona, 1978.

Rostow, Walt W. *The Diffusion of Power: An Essay in Recent History*. New York: Macmillan, 1972.

Rush, Benjamin. *Essays, Literary, Moral and Philosophical*. Philadelphia: *Thomas & Samuel F. Bradford, 1798*.

San Miguel, Guadalupe, Jr. *"Let All of Them Take Heed": Mexican Americans and the Campaign for Educational Equality in Texas, 1910–1981*. Austin: University of Texas Press, 1987.

———. *Black, Not White: School Integration and the Chicano Movement in Houston*. College Station: Texas A&M University Press, 2001.

Shabazz, Amilcar. *Advancing Democracy: African Americans and the Struggle for Access and Equity in Higher Education in Texas*. Chapel Hill: University of North Carolina Press, 2004.

Sitton, Thad, and Milam C. Rowold. *Ringing the Children In: Texas Country Schools*. College Station: Texas A&M University Press, 1987.

Smallwood, James M. *Time of Hope, Time of Despair: Black Texans During Reconstruction*, Series in Ethnic Studies. Port Washington, N.Y.: Kennikat, 1981.

———. *The Feud That Wasn't: The Taylor Ring, Bill Sutton, John Wesley Hardin, and Violence in Texas*. College Station: Texas A&M University Press, 2008.

Smith, Gilbert E. *The Limits of Reform: Politics to Federal Aid to Education, 1937–1950.* New York: Garland, 1982.

Still, Rae Files. *The Gilmer-Aikin Bills: A Study in the Legislative Process.* Austin, Tex.: The Steck Company, 1950.

Tax-Payers' Convention. *Proceedings of the Tax-Payers' Convention of the State of Texas.* Galveston: News Steam Book and Job Office, 1871.

Texas. *Gammel's Laws of Texas.* Austin: Gammel Book Co., 1898.

———. State Board of Education. *Report on the Results of the Texas Statewide School Adequacy Survey.* Austin: Texas State Board of Education, 1937.

———. Legislature. Gilmer-Aikin Committee on Education. *To Have What We Must . . . : A Digest of Proposals to Improve Public Education in Texas.* Austin, 1948.

———. Legislature. House of Representatives. *House Journal,* 51st Leg., R.S. Austin: Texas Legislature, 1949.

———. State Department of Education. *Negro Education in Texas.* Austin: State Department of Education, 1931.

———. Education Association. Texas Commission on Higher Education. *Report to the Honorable Allan Shivers, Governor of Texas and the Legislature of the State of Texas,* November 4, 1954. Austin: Texas Education Association, 1954.

Texas Farmers' Conference. *Proceedings of the Eighteenth Annual Session of the Texas Farmers' Congress in College Station, Texas, August 2–4, 1915.* Austin, Tex.: Von Boeckmann-Jones Co., 1916.

Texas State Historical Association. *Handbook of Texas Online.* http://www.tshaonline.org/handbook/online/.

Tindall, George Brown. *The Emergence of the New South.* Baton Rouge: Louisiana State University Press, 1967.

Tyack, David B. *The One Best System: A History of American Urban Education.* Cambridge, Mass.: Harvard University Press, 1974.

Tyack, David B., and Elisabeth Hansot. *Managers of Virtue: Public School Leadership in America, 1820–1980.* New York: Basic Books, 1982.

Tyack, David B., Robert Lowe, and Elisabeth Hansot. *Public Schools in Hard Times: The Great Depression and Recent Years.* Cambridge, Mass.: Harvard University Press, 1984.

United States. President's Committee on Civil Rights. *"To Secure These Rights": The Report of the President's Committee on Civil Rights.* New York: Simon & Schuster, 1947.

———. "Boundary of Texas, Territory of New Mexico," September 9, 1850. *Statutes at Large and Treaties* 9 (December 1845–March 1851), 446.

———. Department of Health, Education, and Welfare. *The State and Education: The Structure and Control of Public Education at the State Level.* By Fred F. Beach and Robert F. Will. Washington, D.C.: USGPO, 1955.

———. Department of Health, Education, and Welfare. *Public School Finance Programs of the United States.* By Clayon D. Hutchins and Albert R. Munse. Washington, D.C.: USGPO, 1955.

———. Department of the Interior. Office of Education. *The Education of Spanish-Speaking Children in Five Southwestern States.* By Annie Reynolds. Washington D.C.: USGPO, 1933.

———. "Executive Order 9981." July 26, 1948. General Records of the United States Government. RG 11. National Archives.

University of Texas. *Rural School Education: Lectures Delivered and Outlines of Round Tables Held During Rural School Education Week Under the Auspices of the University Summer Schools, July 15–19, 1912.* Bulletin 251. Austin: University of Texas, 1912.

Wallace, Ernest, David M. Vigness, and George B. Ward, eds. *Documents of Texas History,*
2nd ed. Austin: Texas State Historical Association, 2002.

Williams, Patrick G. *Beyond Redemption: Texas Democrats After Reconstruction.* College Station: Texas A&M University Press, 2007.

Wollenberg, Charles M. *All Deliberate Speed: Segregation and Exclusion in California Schools,
1855–1975.* Berkeley: University of California Press, 1978.

Woodward, C. Vann. *Origins of the New South, 1877–1913.* Baton Rouge: Louisiana State
University Press, 1951.

Works, George A. *Texas Educational Survey Report.* Vol. 8. *General Report.* Austin: Texas
Educational Survey Commission, 1925.

## INTERVIEWS

Aikin, Dean. Transcript, August 1, 1974. Aikin, Welma. Transcript, July 10–11, 1974; Gilmer,
Claud. Transcript, November 14–15, 1976; Haskew, Larry. Transcript, August 7, 1978;
Head, J. Manley. Transcript, May 28, 1975; Moore, William. Transcript, Febru-
ary 27, 1975; Sturgeon, L. P. Transcript, January 16, 1976; Taylor, James. Transcript,
March 17, 1976. All interviewed by Corrinne E. Crow. Aikin Special Project. East
Texas State University Oral History Program. James G. Gee Library. Texas A&M
University–Commerce.

Johnson, Lady Bird. Interview. *American Experience. LBJ.* "Part 1–Beautiful Texas." Produced
and directed by Dave Grubin. Videocassette, 60 min. North Texas Public Broadcasting,
Inc., 1991.

Morales, Albert. Interview by C. Herb Skoog. *Reflections* Tape recording no. 330, KGNB-
AM, August 25, 1983. Dittlinger Memorial Library Archives, New Braunfels, Texas.

Nava, Henry. Interview. *School: The Story of American Education.* "Episode 2: As American
As School, 1900–1950." Directed and coproduced by Sarah Mondale. Videocassette, 60
min. Stone Lantern Films, 2001.

Preuss, Isabel Fuentez. Interview by author. Tape recording and transcript, June 23, 1990.
Texas State University–San Marcos.

Smith, Preston. Interview by David Murrah. Tape recording. June 28, 1990. Oral History
Collection. Southwest Collection/Special Collection Libraries, Texas Tech University.

## PERIODICALS

*American Mercury,* 1946.
*Atlantic Monthly,* 1940, 1942.
*Austin American,* 1946–1950, 1981, 1983.
*Dallas Morning News,* 1940–1950, 1981.
*Education for Victory,* 1944–1945.
*Fort Worth Press,* 1940.
*Houston Informer,* 1941–1949.
*Houston Post,* 1981.
*Ladies Home Journal,* 1948.
*Lubbock Avalanche Journal,* 1940–1949, 1981.
*South Atlantic Quarterly,* 1905.

*Texas Observer,* 1950.
*Texas Outlook,* 1924–1954.
*Time,* 1937.

### UNPUBLISHED MATERIAL

Arredondo, Santos Torres. "A Survey of Special Methods and Procedures for Teaching English to Spanish-Speaking Children." Master's thesis, Southwest Texas State Teachers College, 1943.  ·

Baenziger, Ann Patton. "Bold Beginnings: The Radical Program in Texas, 1870–1873." Master's thesis, Southwest Texas State University, 1970.

Darden, Otis M. "The Integration of Afro-Americans into the Army Mainstream, 1948–1954." Master's thesis, U.S. Army Command and General Staff College, 1993.

Davis, Frances T. "The Role of Senator A. M. Aikin, Jr., in the Development of Public Education in Texas, 1932–1974." EdD diss., East Texas State University, 1975.

Elliott, Horace Carl. "L. A. Woods: State Superintendent of Public Instruction in Texas." Master's thesis, Hardin-Simmons University, 1947.

Kite, Jodella D. "A Social History of the Anglo-American Colonies in Mexican Texas, 1821–1835." PhD diss., Texas Tech University, 1990.

Moore, Hollis Andrew. "Equalization of Educational Opportunity and the Distribution of State School Funds in Texas." EdD diss., University of Texas, 1947.

Parr, Eunice Elvira. "A Comparative Study of Mexican and American Children in the Schools of San Antonio, Texas." Master's thesis, University of Chicago, 1926; reprint, San Francisco: R and E Research Associates, 1971.

Sosebee, M. Scott. "The Split in the Texas Democratic Party, 1936–1956." Master's thesis, Texas Tech University, 2000.

Stiles, Jo Ann Pankratz. "The Changing Economic and Educational Status of Texas Negroes, 1940–1960." Master's thesis, University of Texas, 1966.

Tinsley, James A. "The Progressive Movement in Texas." PhD diss., University of Wisconsin, 1953.

Velarde, Karen A. "A Teacher's Tale: The Diary of Nannie Dorroh Odom, 1894–1904." Master's thesis, Texas Tech University, 1993.

# INDEX

ISBN-13: 978-1-60344-111-7
ISBN-10: 1-60344-111-5